PAPER PUPS

PAPER PUPS

35 DOGS TO COPY, CUT & FOLD

Hiroshi Hayakawa

LARK CRAFTS
Asheville

LARK CRAFTS

An Imprint of Sterling Publishing
387 Park Avenue South
New York, NY 10016

ISBN 978-1-4547-0392-1

Library of Congress Cataloging-in-Publication Data

Hayakawa, Hiroshi, 1962-
  Paper pups : 35 dogs to copy, cut & fold / Hiroshi Hayakawa. -- First Edition.
    pages cm
  ISBN 978-1-4547-0392-1 (pbk.)
  1. Paper work. 2. Dogs in art. I. Title.
  TT870.H3825 2013
  745.54--dc23
                            2012030563

Distributed in Canada by Sterling Publishing
c/o Canadian Manda Group, 165 Dufferin Street
Toronto, Ontario, Canada M6K 3H6
Distributed in the United Kingdom by GMC Distribution Services
Castle Place, 166 High Street, Lewes, East Sussex, England BN7 1XU
Distributed in Australia by Capricorn Link (Australia) Pty. Ltd.
P.O. Box 704, Windsor, NSW 2756, Australia

For information about custom editions, special sales, and premium and corporate purchases, please
contact Sterling Special Sales at 800-805-5489 or specialsales@sterlingpublishing.com.

Email academic@larkbooks.com for information about desk and examination copies.
The complete policy can be found at larkcrafts.com.

Every effort has been made to ensure that all the information in this book is accurate. However, due
to differing conditions, tools, and individual skills, the publisher cannot be responsible for any injuries,
losses, and other damages that may result from the use of the information in this book.

Manufactured in China

2 4 6 8 10 9 7 5 3 1

larkcrafts.com

Contents

The Dogs

Very Easy ● ○ ○ ○

Easy ● ● ○ ○

Intermediate ● ● ● ○

Advanced ● ● ● ●

Dog Accessories

Dedication

This book is dedicated to all my canine family members past and present: Puggy, Peanut, Pearl, Little Petey, Bettina, and Ernie.

Introduction

We all love dogs, don't we? They are companions in life. They don't care what job you hold, how rich or poor you are. They give you unconditional love no matter what. All they want is to be with you and play with you.

For many years, I've had this dream project of writing a paper craft book about dogs. With such an array of distinctive breeds and appearances, they're very exciting to design. Dog lovers (and there are so many of us!) are familiar with the unique traits and expressions of individual dog breeds. It's often those features and mannerisms that make us fall in love with particular types of dogs. When people see my work and can instantly identify a pup's breed, it gives me great creative joy. Above all, however, this project is my humble way of expressing gratitude to our canine companions for being just who they are, for teaching us humans what it's like to love and to be loved, and ultimately showing us how truly precious life is when shared with them.

All the projects in this book were designed using two types of traditional paper craft techniques: origami and kirigami. Origami means "paper folding" and kirigami means "paper cutting" in Japanese. In this book, I will show you how to combine these two techniques to create dogs that are three-dimensional and full of details. These techniques involve three very distinct processes: scoring, cutting, and folding. That's right. You don't have to use glue or tape to make these dogs. They all have interlocking joints that give them enough structural strength to stand alone without the use of adhesive.

Before you pick up a pair of scissors and start cutting, however, read the section "How to Use This Book." The process for each dog design is the same: photocopy the project template and follow the step-by-step instructions and illustrations to score, cut, fold, and shape it into a dimensional (and expressive) pup. Some of the projects might look a bit intimidating at first, but you'll discover that the process of carefully shaping paper is actually quite simple and even meditative. So familiarize yourself first with the basic steps, and then begin creating.

The projects in this book are grouped by skill level: very easy, easy, intermediate, and advanced. If you are new to kirigami, I suggest you start with the easiest dog projects before you work your way up to the more complex ones.

I have also included templates for various accessories and amusing items (such as a sweater for the Chihuahua and a bow for the Shih Tzu), so you can have fun dressing them up! Other extras are online at www.larkcrafts.com: make a long fur version of the Yorkshire Terrier as a companion for the spiky fur Yorkie in the book, or make 101 puppies for the Dalmatian family!

I had a blast working on this book. I hope you enjoy making these dogs as much as I enjoyed designing them, and that they keep you company for years to come.

How to Use This Book

You might think that creating 35 projects out of paper would require quite the collection of techniques and tools, but the reality is rather simple: each of these pups is made by scoring, cutting, folding, and shaping paper, and you'll need only a few basic tools to get going! This section of the book thoroughly explores basic kirigami techniques as well as some tips to help you along the way. The projects' step-by-step illustrations and templates include symbols that explain where to cut, fold, and so on, and you'll find a descriptive explanation of those symbols in the following pages. While the construction of each dog is based on its physical shape and traits, you're the artist when it comes to adding color and detail to your paper pup. Feel free to reference the project photos for color inspiration, or personalize your dog with the markings and patterns of your preference.

WORKING WITH THE TEMPLATES

Every project in this book begins with a full-size template, found on pages 108–142. Keep in mind that the template details are meant to be printed on the reverse side (or underside) of your paper: make sure you score and cut on the printed side. Once you've constructed the dogs, most of the printed folding lines won't be visible on their outer surfaces.

Photocopy the templates instead of using the originals. This way, you will be able to make as many dogs as you like. You can give a special family to the dog of your choice. How about turning your desktop into a dog park where different breeds of dogs can spend time together in peace? Maybe you should have your own dog show! The possibilities are endless.

You will also find templates of special display items in this book, including a fire hydrant and a doghouse. Of course, you can improvise and come up with your own unique landscapes. Be creative in displaying your favorite dogs.

Check out www.larkcrafts.com for templates of the dog variations, such as a Yorkie with long fur or a Great Dane with droopy ears.

PAPER

Creating dimensional paper projects requires using paper thin enough to be easily folded yet sturdy enough to give structural strength to freestanding dogs. With this in mind, you'll need to copy the project templates onto cardstock rather than basic paper. All of the projects in *Paper Pups* were made with cardstock, which you can easily find at your local office supply or craft store.

There are a variety of cardstock thicknesses, colors, shades, and textures to choose from. Stay away from inexpensive cardstock that may have a white core in the center; when you score and fold it, the white core will appear in your fold. To photocopy or print on cardstock, adjust the printer's paper setting and, depending on your printer, you might want to hand feed the paper one sheet at a time to avoid jamming.

SYMBOLS

As you work on the projects, you'll need to understand the symbols that appear on the templates and in the illustrations that come with the assembly instructions. These are shown and described below.

A transition from one step to the next

Move a part of the template or a tool in the direction of the arrow

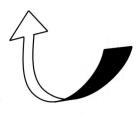

Movement occurs toward/on the reverse side of the template

Turn over a part of the template, reversing the inside/outside relationship

Create a rounded surface with a dowel

Create a curved surface with a dowel. The shape of the arrow indicates the general shape and the direction of the curve.

Enlarged view of a smaller section

Indicates ups and downs of the surface levels after a series of folds

Turn over the entire template.

SCORING

Scoring is the act of creating lines and edges in paper that will facilitate folding and shaping: it is the first step in making any of these projects (yes, even before cutting out a template). You'll score the folding lines first, which are indicated by dashed and dotted lines on a template.

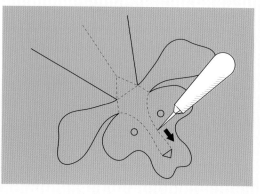

Scoring makes folding easier and neater later on. If you cut out the template first, scoring these lines, especially in a small, delicate area, is sometimes more difficult, so it's best to score first.

Begin by placing the template on a smooth, flat, hard surface. A surface that's too soft, such as newspaper, may cause you to dig deep grooves into the template as you score, which would make the assembled dog unsightly.

The key to successful scoring is to avoid exerting too much pressure on your scoring tool. Score the folding lines with an awl, a small nail, a bone folder, a ballpoint pen that's run out of ink, or anything else with a hard, pointed tip. Even though some of the scored lines will be folded downward and others will be folded upward, score them all on the same printed side of the template. Try not to stray from the marked lines.

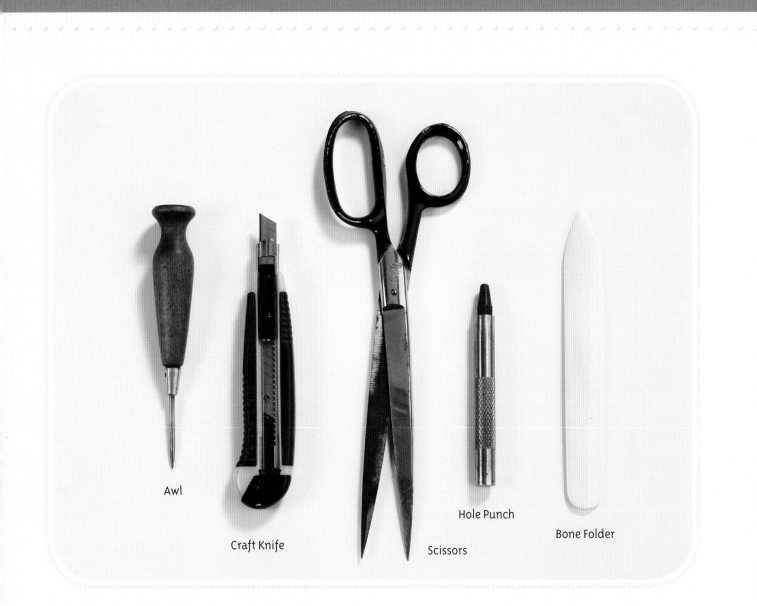

Awl

Craft Knife

Scissors

Hole Punch

Bone Folder

To make scoring straight lines easier, use the edge of a ruler as a guide.

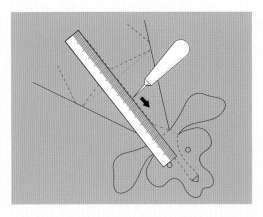

CUTTING

After you've scored the folding lines, you'll begin cutting. The solid lines on the templates represent the cutting lines.

First, use a craft knife to cut along all the solid lines within the interior perimeter of the template. These lines include small cuts along the eyelids, the opening of the nose on some of the dogs, and the tabs for interlocking joints. When making small, curved cuts such as those for the eyelids, rotate the paper in the opposite direction as the movement of your knife.

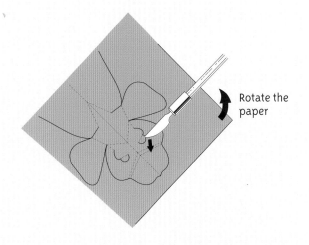

Rotate the paper

Be very careful when using a craft knife; keep your hand away from the path of the blade. A small child may need an adult's help when making precision cuts.

Next, use a pair of scissors or a craft knife to cut along the contour perimeter of the template.

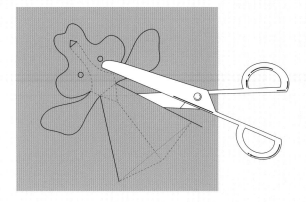

When cutting away small, sharp areas that extend beyond the template's contour but toward the interior (the German Shepherd's cheeks shown below is a good example), first use scissors to make a rough cut, **Ⓐ** and then cut away the remaining paper with a craft knife, moving the instrument from the interior toward the exterior. **Ⓑ** Remove the template from the page.

Ⓐ

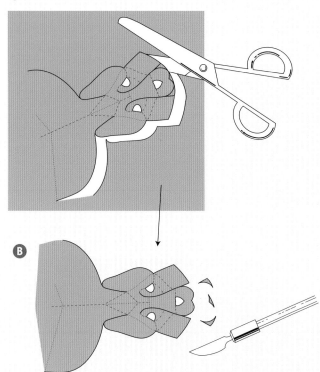

Ⓑ

Cutting a straight line is easy. Use the edge of a ruler as a guide—the same as when you are scoring a straight line— and cut along the line with a craft knife. Use a metal ruler so that you don't damage its edge with the blade.

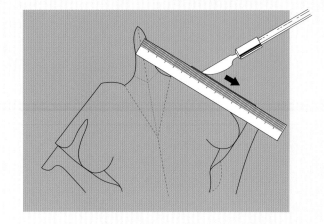

To cut out small circles such as the eyes of the Weimaraner (page 20), you can use a craft knife, but the best tool for this job is a paper (or a leather) punch.

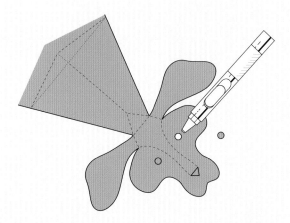

Align the tip of the punch with the circle you are cutting out, and gently tap the end of the tool with a wooden or rubber mallet.

FOLDING

Now that you've scored and cut out the project template, you'll begin the really fun part: folding. This is when the dog actually begins to take shape into a dimensional object. Two types of folds are used in this book: the *peak fold* and the *valley fold*. A peak fold is represented by a dotted line, a valley by a line of dashes. Most folding can be done with your fingers, but small, delicate sections will require a little help from some tools.

Making a Peak Fold

Use the index finger and the thumb of one hand to push down on both sides of the dotted line while simultaneously pushing up the area under and along the folding line with the index finger of your other hand.

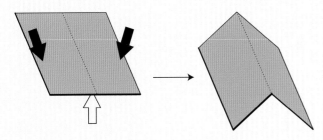

If the section of the template that calls for this type of fold is too small to use the edge of your finger, use a small tool, such as a toothpick, a needle, or the awl that you used for scoring.

Making a Valley Fold

Use one finger to push down along the dashed line of the template while pushing up along both sides of the folding line with the index finger and the thumb of your other hand. Again, if the section to be folded is too small for your finger, push down the folding line with a small scoring tool instead.

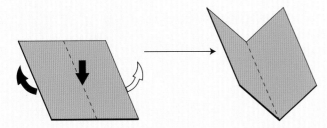

Folding a Curved Line

To fold a curved line that isn't straight, use your thumb and index finger to pinch and squeeze along opposing sides of the folding line while pushing the area under and along the folding line with the index finger of your other hand.

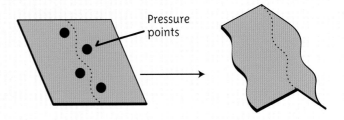

Pressure points

Making a Pocket Fold

Pocket folding—a combination of a peak fold and a valley fold—is typically used to form the neck-shoulder and tail-hip connections of many dogs in this book. The figure below illustrates how to make this fold.

SHAPING

These projects are designed to capture each dog's unique pose and expression, and some require the use of a few simple shaping techniques. These techniques aren't applicable to all the dogs in this book, but using them adds an extra sense of realism and character to your work.

The first technique is used to round the body of a dog. After cutting out the template, turn it over. Use one hand to press the template against the edge of a desk or table and use the other hand to pull it back and forth across the edge a couple of times. This will add a natural curve to the dog's body.

To create a nice, smooth curve in a small area of a template, roll it over a dowel. **A B** A dowel produces a much neater result than rolling the template with your fingers. If you don't have a dowel, substitute a round pencil or any other thin, tubular object.

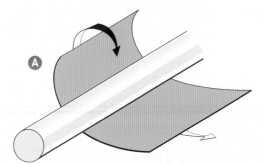

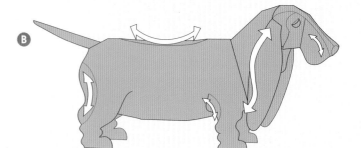

Many of the dogs in this book are held together by means of interlocking joints. They make it possible to assemble the dogs without using glue or tape and provide them with enough strength to make them freestanding. And all the dogs in this book are freestanding. When a project is completed, the last step is to adjust the angles of the legs so that the dog will stand comfortably on his paws without falling over.

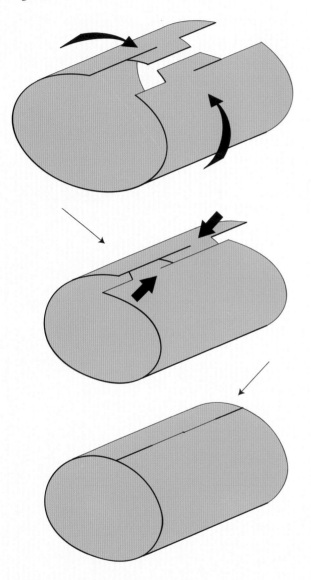

COLORING

From a Dalmatian's spots to a Siberian Husky's piercing blue eyes, the markings of some dog breeds are very distinctive. Many of the projects in the following pages feature multiple versions of each pup, and I have included some variations of color and pattern in an effort to recognize the range of a breed's appearance. Reference the project photos for breed-specific markings, or personalize your pup by adding your own color and detail. Remember, too, that you can be creative with your paper color choice: how about a paisley Weimaraner or a bubblegum pink Poodle?

You can use any opaque paint or drawing medium, as long as it isn't oil based. Acrylic paint, poster paint, colored pencils, and pastels will all work just fine.

SELECTING A DOG

The projects in *Paper Pups* range in skill level from Very Easy to Advanced, and while they all employ the same basic techniques, it's always a good idea to practice a bit before diving right into a challenging or intricate design. If you're new to paper cutting and folding crafts, I recommend getting your feet wet by starting with the Very Easy category and gradually moving on to more detailed dogs as you develop your skills.

Bichon Frise

With a fluffy, curled double coat, a Bichon Frise is
sometimes affectionately compared to a cotton ball.
With a merry temperament and inquisitive nature,
they make great companions.

1 Using the Bichon Frise template on page 111, score the folding lines, then cut along all the solid lines, including the eyelids and the tabs for the interlocking joints, as depicted in "How to Use This Book" on pages 7–13.

2 Pull the two halves of the lower jaw together **A**.

3 Interlock the jaw joint by crossing the tabs. Round the head by rolling it over a dowel **B**.

4 Pull up the eyelids. Fold down the neck behind the head **C**.

5 Pocket fold the neck, the shoulders, and the tail. Raise the tail **D** **E**.

6 Round the chest by rolling it over a dowel. Interlock the joint by crossing the tabs **F** **G**.

7 Round the muzzle by rolling it over a dowel. Make the body round. Fold the hind legs following the scored lines, and then curl the tail a little **H** **I**.

8 The Bichon Frise featured in this project photo has no added color or embellishment. Feel free to personalize your Bichon Frise and add painted detail if you wish.

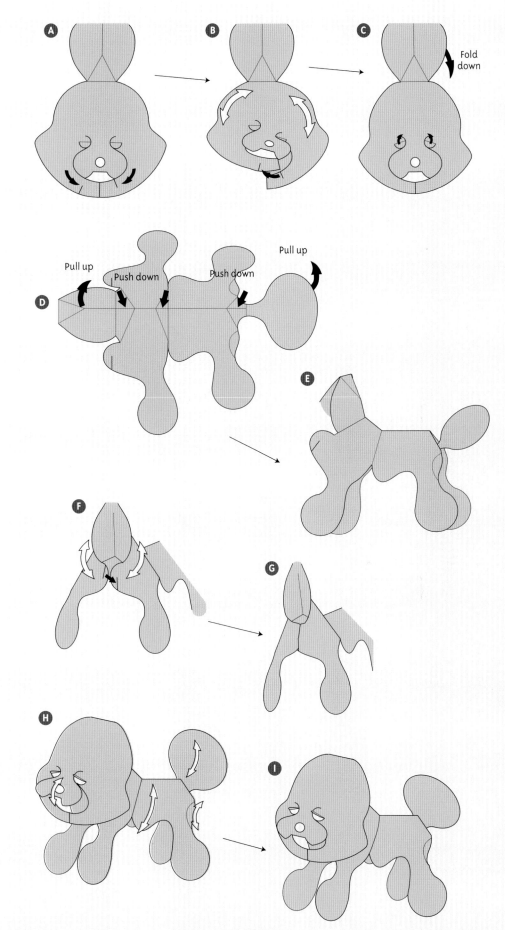

Dalmatian

Throughout history, this spotted fellow has had many jobs, including "coach dog" or "carriage dog," which required him to run alongside and guard horse-drawn carriages. As a result, the Dalmatian's affinity for horses still exists today.

BONUS PROJECT
available FREE at
www.larkcrafts.com/bonus

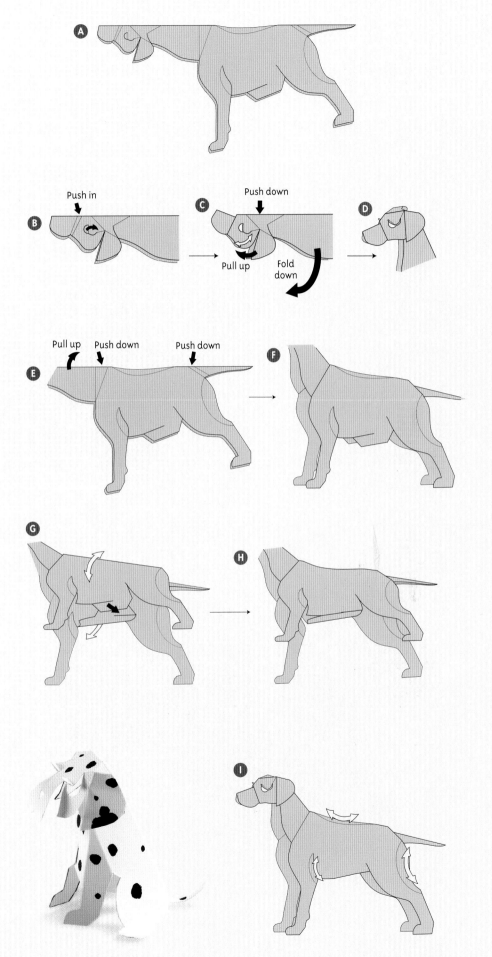

1 Using the Dalmatian template on page 122, score the folding lines, then cut along all the solid lines, including the eyelids and the tabs for the interlocking joint, as depicted in "How to Use This Book" on pages 7–13.

2 Fold the template in half by following the scored centerline **A**.

3 Pull up the eyelids. Push in the muzzle and fold its top end under the eyes **B**.

4 Round the cheeks by rolling them over a small dowel. Swing the bottom of the ears toward the cheeks. Fold down the neck behind the head while you valley fold the top of the head **C D**.

5 Pocket fold the neck into the shoulders, and the tail into the hips **E F**.

6 Round the body by rolling it over a dowel. Interlock the stomach joint by crossing the tabs **G H**.

7 Push down the back to add more curve to it. Fold the front and hind legs following the scored lines **I**.

8 Add color and pattern to your Dalmatian by referencing the project photos.

TIP

Want to create a roly-poly Dalmatian puppy (or a pack of puppies)? Head to www.larkcrafts.com/bonus for a downloadable template and how-to instructions.

Scottish Terrier

With a feisty blend of charm and spirit, the Scottie is a happy, determined creature nicknamed "the Diehard" for his often stubborn and rugged manner.

1 Using the Scottish Terrier template on page 137, score the folding lines, then cut along all the solid lines, including the eyebrows and the tabs for the interlocking joint, as depicted in "How to Use This Book" on pages 7–13.

2 Fold the template in half by following the scored centerline Ⓐ.

3 Push down the muzzle and pocket fold it under the eyebrows Ⓑ.

4 Push down the cheeks and pull up the ears. Fold down the neck behind the head while you valley fold the top of the head Ⓒ Ⓓ.

5 Pocket fold the neck and the tail Ⓔ Ⓕ.

6 Interlock the chest joint by crossing the tabs. Pinch and squeeze the ears Ⓖ.

7 Pull out the ears to the sides. Round the neck by rolling it over a dowel. Add more curve to the back by pushing it down Ⓗ.

TIP

The Scotties featured in this project photo have no added color or embellishment. Simply change the paper color to reflect the different coat colors among the Scottish Terrier breed.

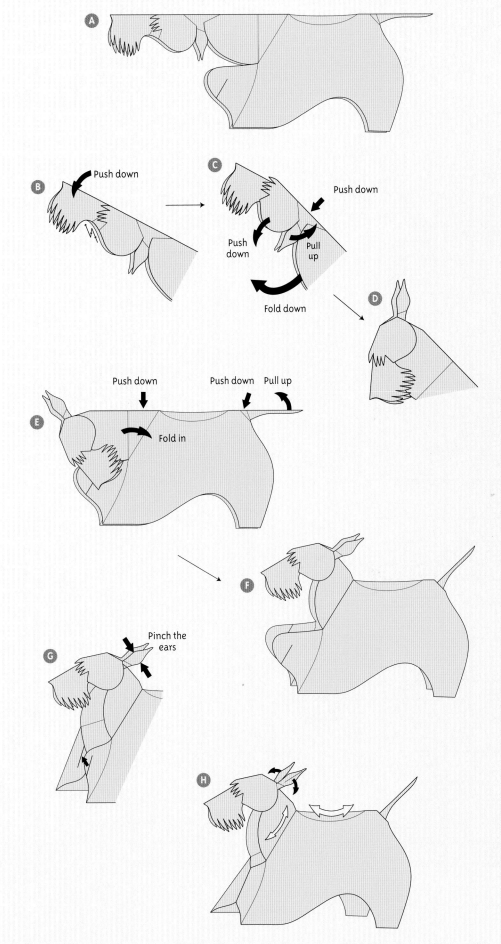

Weimaraner

Mix equal parts elegance and playfulness, and you've got a Weimaraner. Their sleek profiles and glossy gray coats combine with great intelligence and a love of energetic fun.

1 Using the Weimaraner template on page 141, score the folding lines, then cut along all the solid lines, including the eyes and the nose, as depicted in "How to Use This Book" on pages 7–13.

2 Fold down the cheeks. Round the muzzle by rolling it over a dowel and squeeze in the top of the muzzle. Fold down the ears over the cheeks **A B**.

3 Fold the body in half by following the scored centerline **C**.

4 Pocket fold the neck into the shoulders, and the tail into the hips. Shape the front legs by folding along the scored lines and by adding more curves to them **D E**.

TIP

The Weimaraners featured in this project photo have no added color or embellishment. Simply change the paper color to reflect the different coat colors among this dog's breed.

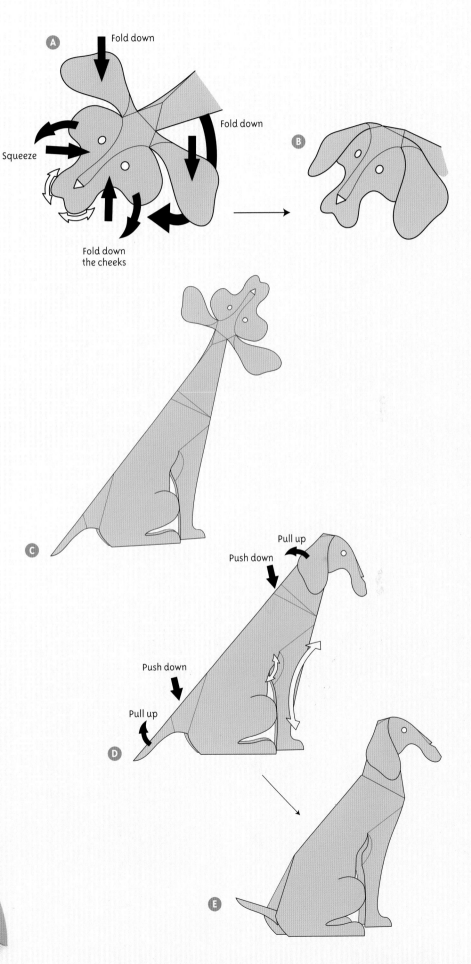

Beagle

Known for its excellent sense of smell, the Beagle is a friendly, cheerful fellow, often relied upon for hunting and sporting events. You're probably familiar with a very famous Beagle: Snoopy from the comic strip "Peanuts"!

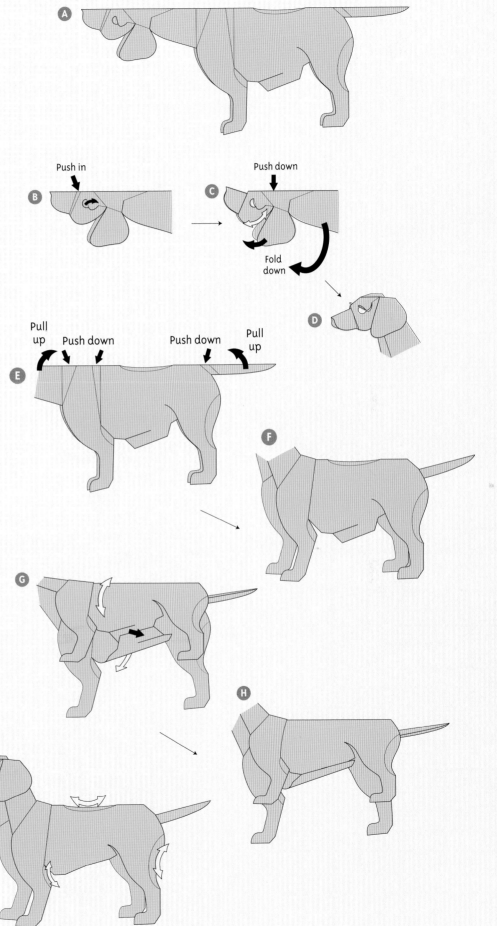

1. Using the Beagle template on page 110, score the folding lines, then cut along all the solid lines, including the eyelids, the nose, and the tabs for the interlocking joint, as depicted in "How to Use This Book" on pages 7–13.

2. Fold the template in half by following the scored centerline **A**.

3. Pull up the eyelids. Push up the muzzle and fold its top end under the eyes **B**.

4. Round the cheeks. Swing the ears to the front. Fold down the neck behind the head while you valley fold the top of the head **C D**.

5. Pocket fold the neck, the shoulders, and the tail **E F**.

6. Round the body by rolling it over a dowel. Interlock the stomach joint by crossing the tabs **G H**.

7. Add more of a curve to the back by pushing it down. Fold the front and hind legs, following the scored lines **I**.

8. Add color and pattern to your Beagle by referencing the project photo.

Push in   Push down

Fold down

Pull up   Push down   Push down   Pull up

Afghan Hound

The exotic-looking Afghan Hound is known for its long silky hair, graceful features, and curled tail. Her dignified appearance is balanced with an athletic, friendly nature.

1 Using the Afghan Hound template on page 108, score the folding lines, then cut along all the solid lines, including the eyelids, the lines in the fur, and the tabs for the interlocking joint, as depicted in "How to Use This Book" on pages 7–13.

2 Fold the template in half by following the scored centerline **A**.

3 Pull down the muzzle. Add curves to the sides of the nose. Fold down the neck behind the head while you valley fold the top of the head **B**.

4 Pull up the eyelids **C D**.

5 Pocket fold the neck and the tail **E F**.

6 Interlock the chest joint by crossing the tabs **G**.

7 Push down the back and add more curve to it. Round the neck by rolling it over a dowel. Squeeze the front and the hind legs so that your Afghan Hound will stand up comfortably on the ground **H**.

TIP

The Afghan Hound featured in this project photo has a simple black nose and no other embellishment. Feel free to personalize your Afghan Hound and add painted detail if you wish.

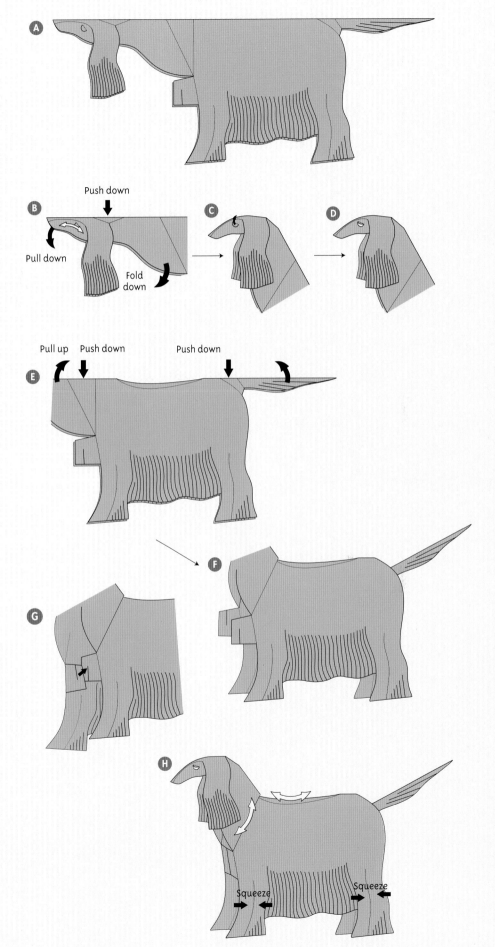

Boxer

Bright, sweet, and playful, the Boxer is a loving friend and loyal family member with great personality and a heart of gold. Squeaky toys, a soft bed, and human affection are her top priorities.

BONUS PROJECT
available FREE at
www.larkcrafts.com/bonus

1 Using the Boxer template on page 114, score the folding lines, then cut along all the solid lines, including the eyelids, the nose, and the tabs for the interlocking joints, as depicted in "How to Use This Book" on pages 7–13.

2 Pull up the eyelids. Push down the bases of the ears and fold them behind the head. Pull up the muzzle toward the eyes. Fold down the cheeks **A**.

3 Fold down the neck behind the head while you valley fold the top of the head **B**.

4 Pinch and squeeze the ears **C D**.

5 Fold the body in half by following the scored centerline. Pocket fold the neck and the tail **E F**.

6 Round the body by rolling it over a dowel. Interlock the stomach joint by crossing the tabs **G H**.

7 Add more curve to the back by pushing it down. Fold the front and the hind legs by following the scored lines **I**.

8 Add color and pattern to your Boxer by referencing the project photo.

TIP

So you'd like to make your Boxer with soft, un-cropped ears? Capture that sweet expressiveness by visiting www.larkcrafts.com/bonus for a downloadable template, and follow the same instructions above to make a soft-eared Boxer.

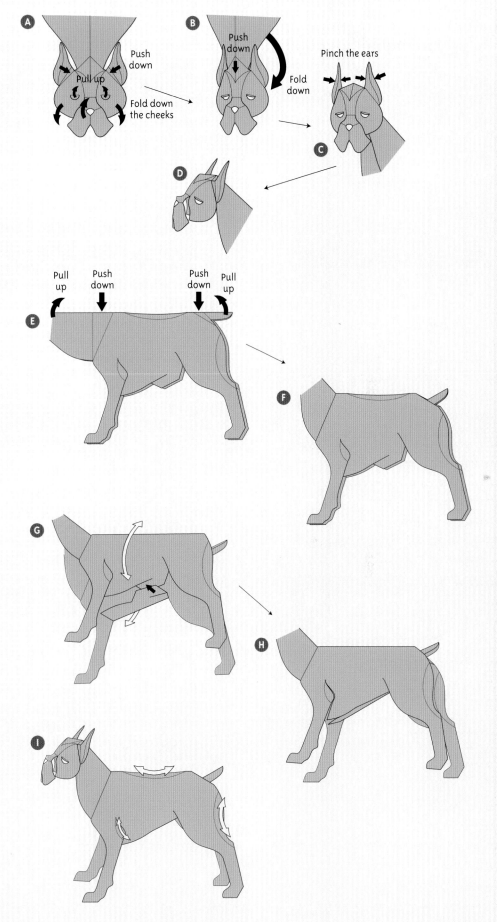

Bull Terrier

Bull Terriers are instantly recognizable by their egg-shaped heads and tank-like bodies. Underneath their gladiator appearance, they're sweet, goofy, and fun-loving pals.

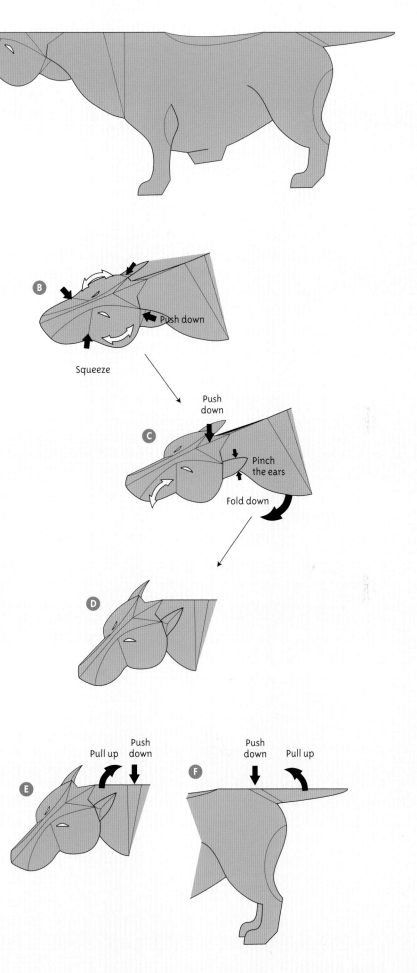

1 Using the Bull Terrier template on page 115, score the folding lines, then cut along all the solid lines, including the eyes and the tabs for the interlocking joint, as depicted in "How to Use This Book" on pages 7–13.

2 Fold the template in half by following the scored centerline Ⓐ.

3 Push down the bases of the ears and fold them behind the head. Round the cheeks. Squeeze in the sides of the muzzle Ⓑ.

4 Pinch the ears. Add curves to the sides of the muzzle. Fold down the neck behind the head while you valley fold the top of the head Ⓒ Ⓓ.

5 Pocket fold the neck and the tail Ⓔ Ⓕ.

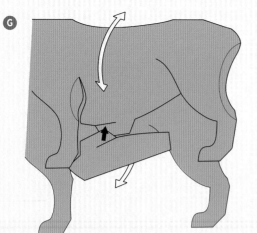

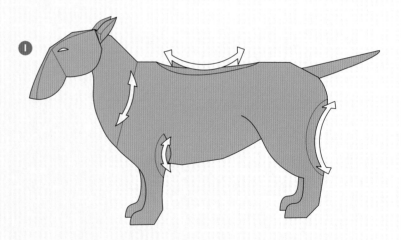

6 Round the body by rolling it over a dowel. Interlock the stomach joint by crossing the tabs **G** **H**.

7 Round the shoulders by rolling them over a dowel. Add more curve to the back by pushing it down. Fold the front and the hind legs by following the scored lines **I**.

8 Add color and pattern to your Bull Terrier by referencing the project photos.

Collie

With a long, graceful face and lovely flowing fur, the Collie has both beauty and brains—they're highly intelligent and make gentle, loyal companions.

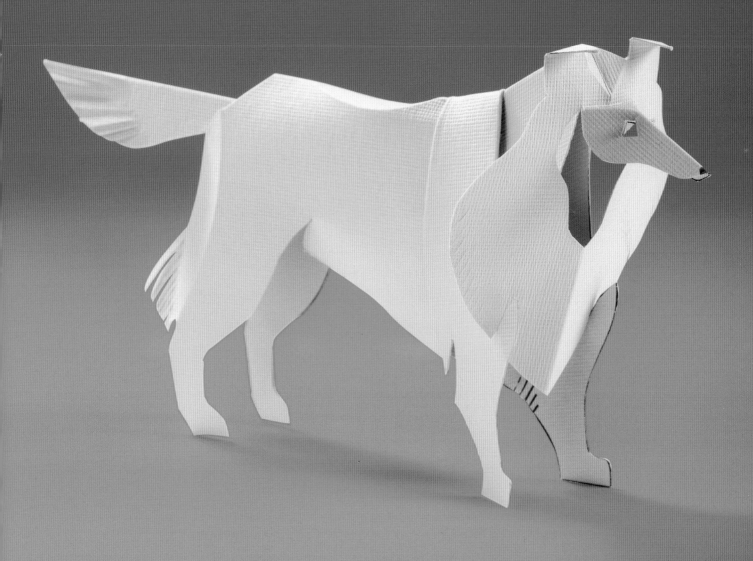

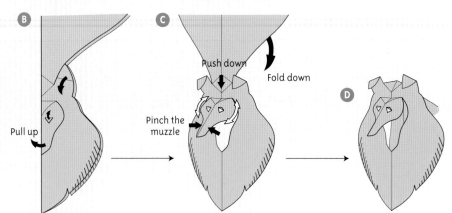

1 Using the Collie template on page 119, score the folding lines, then cut along all the solid lines, including the eyelids, the lines in the fur, and the tabs for the interlocking joints, as depicted in "How to Use This Book" on pages 7–13.

2 Fold the template in half by following the scored centerline Ⓐ.

3 Fold down the ears. Pull up the eyelids and the muzzle Ⓑ.

4 Pinch and squeeze the muzzle. Round the cheek lines. Fold down the neck behind the head while you valley fold the top of the head Ⓒ Ⓓ.

5 Pocket fold the neck, the shoulders, and the tail Ⓔ Ⓕ.

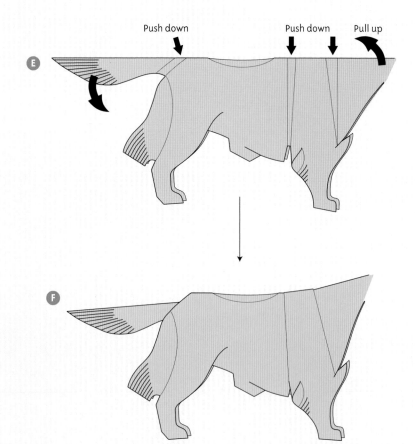

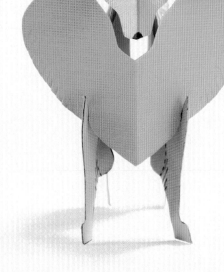

6 Round the body by rolling it over a dowel. Interlock the stomach joint by crossing the tabs **G** **H**.

7 Lower the head and interlock the notches at the bottom of the chest fur with the cuts made in the front legs. Add more curve to the back by pushing it down. Round the shoulders and add more curve to the hind legs by rolling them over a dowel. Fold the front and the hind legs by following the scored lines **I**.

TIP

The Collie featured in these project photos has a simple black nose and no other embellishment, but feel free to personalize your Collie and add painted detail if you wish.

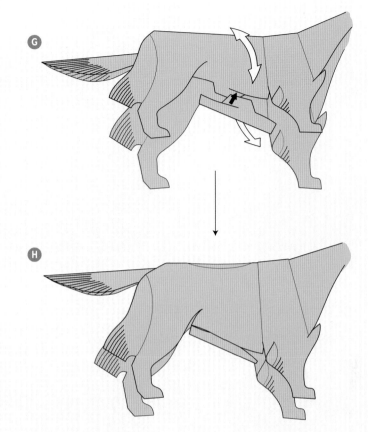

Add more curve to the hind legs

Round the shoulders

Dachshund

They may look like funny little hot dogs, but Dachshunds are fiercely loyal with a keen sense of curiosity, always ready for playtime.

1 Using the Dachshund template on page 121, score the folding lines, then cut along all the solid lines, including the eyelids and the tabs for the interlocking joint, as depicted in "How to Use This Book" on pages 7–13.

2 Fold the template in half by following the scored centerline **A**.

3 Pull up the eyelids. Fold the bases of the ears and swing them over the cheeks. Push up the muzzle and fold its top end under the eyes. Fold down the neck behind the head while you valley fold the top of the head **B**.

4 Push in the cheeks behind the eyes **C**.

5 Pocket fold the neck, the shoulders and the tail **D** **E**.

6 Round the body by rolling it over a dowel. Interlock the stomach joint by crossing the tabs **F** **G**.

7 Add more curve to the back by pushing it down. Round the shoulders. Fold the front and the hind legs by following the scored lines **H**.

TIP
The Dachshunds featured in this project photo have simple black noses and no other embellishment, but feel free to personalize your Dachshund and add painted detail if you wish.

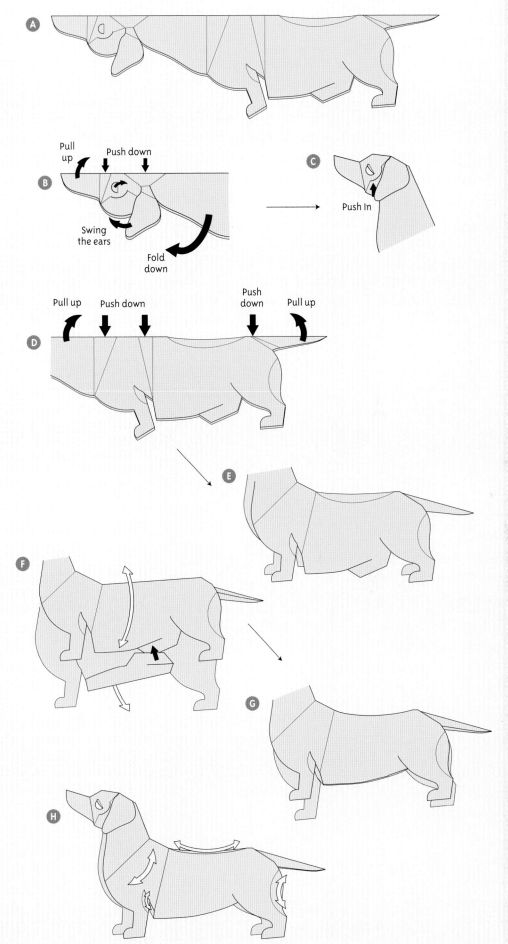

Doberman Pinscher

Talk about a distinguished appearance! The highly intelligent and loving Doberman Pinscher is known for his devotion to family and playful nature.

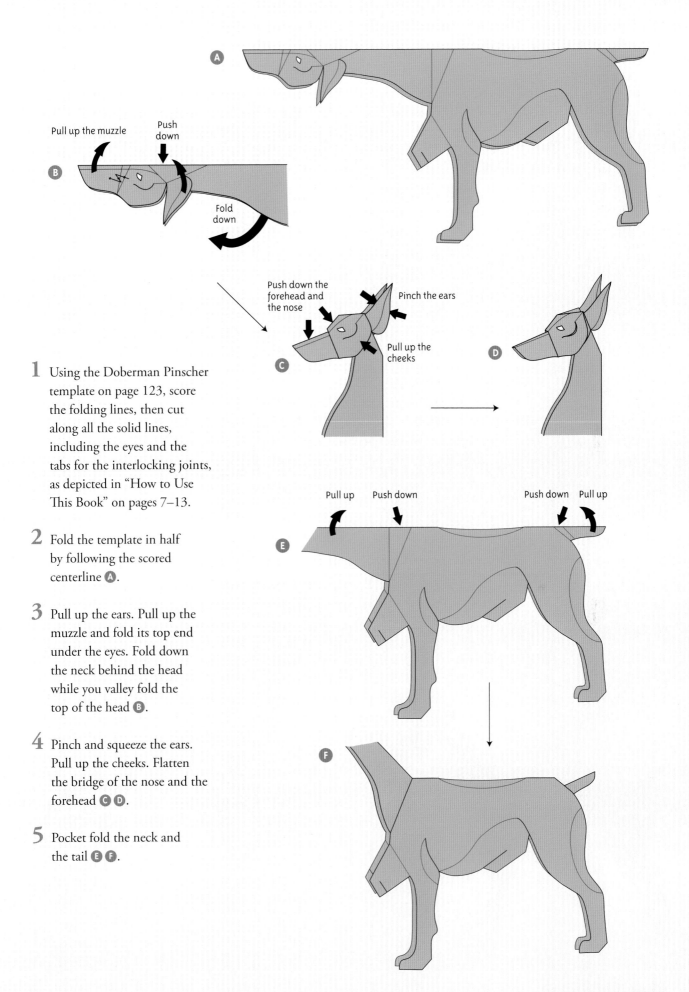

Pull up the muzzle

Push down

Fold down

Push down the forehead and the nose

Pinch the ears

Pull up the cheeks

Pull up Push down

Push down Pull up

1 Using the Doberman Pinscher template on page 123, score the folding lines, then cut along all the solid lines, including the eyes and the tabs for the interlocking joints, as depicted in "How to Use This Book" on pages 7–13.

2 Fold the template in half by following the scored centerline Ⓐ.

3 Pull up the ears. Pull up the muzzle and fold its top end under the eyes. Fold down the neck behind the head while you valley fold the top of the head Ⓑ.

4 Pinch and squeeze the ears. Pull up the cheeks. Flatten the bridge of the nose and the forehead Ⓒ Ⓓ.

5 Pocket fold the neck and the tail Ⓔ Ⓕ.

6 Interlock the stomach joint by crossing the tabs **G** **H**.

7 Interlock the chest joint by crossing the tabs **I**.

8 Push down the back and add more curve to it. Fold the front and the hind legs by following the scored lines **J**.

9 Add color and pattern to your Doberman Pinscher by referencing the project photos.

German Shepherd

Known as the world's leading police, guard, and military dog, the German Shepherd is also a calm and loving family companion, often relied upon as a seeing eye dog.

1 Using the German Shepherd template on page 126, score the folding lines, then cut along all the solid lines, including the eyes, the nose, and the tabs for the interlocking joints, as depicted in "How to Use This Book" on pages 7–13.

2 Fold down the ears forward. Fold down the cheeks. Pull up the muzzle toward the eyes **A**.

3 Push the eyes back **B**.

4 Fold down the neck behind the head while you valley fold the top of the head **C**

5 Shape the ears by squeezing them **D**.

6 Fold the body in half by following the scored centerline. Pocket fold the neck, the shoulders, and push down the tail **E** **F**.

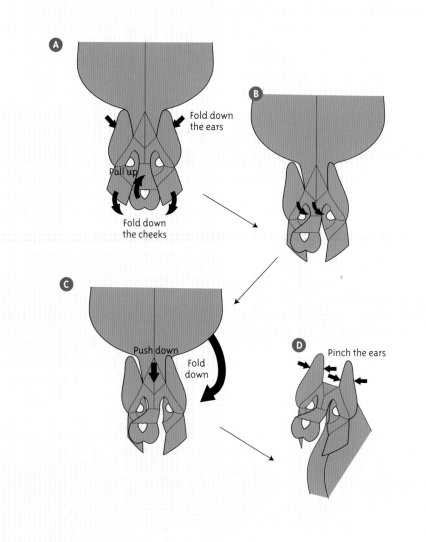

A Fold down the ears
Pull up
Fold down the cheeks

B

C Push down
Fold down

D Pinch the ears

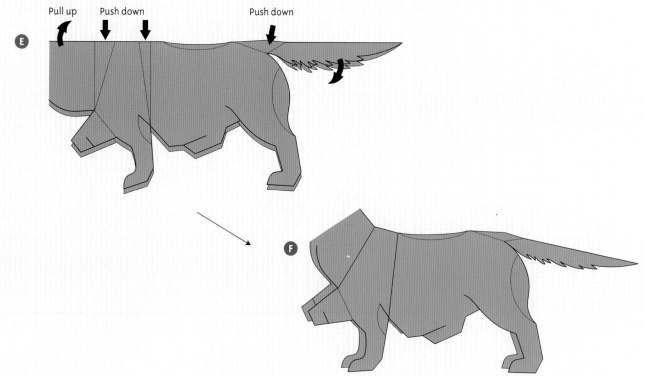

E Pull up Push down Push down

F

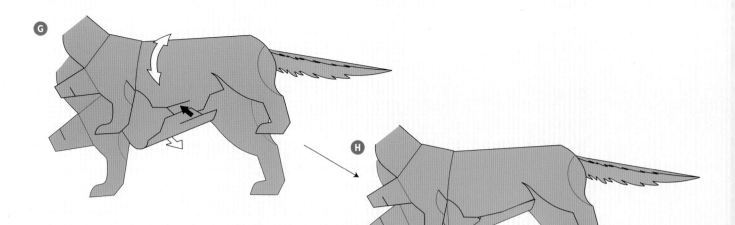

7 Round the body by rolling it over a dowel. Interlock the stomach joint by crossing the tabs **G** **H**.

8 Interlock the chest joint by crossing the tabs **I**.

9 Push down the back and add more curve to it. Fold the front and the hind legs by following the scored lines **J**.

10 Add color and pattern to your German Shepherd by referencing the project photos.

Jack Russell Terrier

Bursting with lively energy and agile enthusiasm, the Jack Russell Terrier is ready for you to throw that ball *right now*, if you please.

1 Using the Jack Russell Terrier template on page 130, score the folding lines, then cut along all the solid lines, including the eyes, the nose, and the tabs for the interlocking joint, as depicted in "How to Use This Book" on pages 7–13.

2 Fold down the ears over the head. Fold down the cheeks. Squeeze in the muzzle **A**.

3 Fold down the neck behind the head while you valley fold the top of the head **B** **C**.

4 Fold the body in half by following the scored centerline. Pocket fold the neck, the shoulders, and the tail **D** **E**.

5 Round the body by rolling it over a dowel. Interlock the stomach joint by crossing the tabs **F** **G**.

6 Add more curve to the back by pushing it down. Fold the front and hind legs, following the scored lines **H**.

7 Add color and pattern to your Jack Russell Terrier by referencing the project photo.

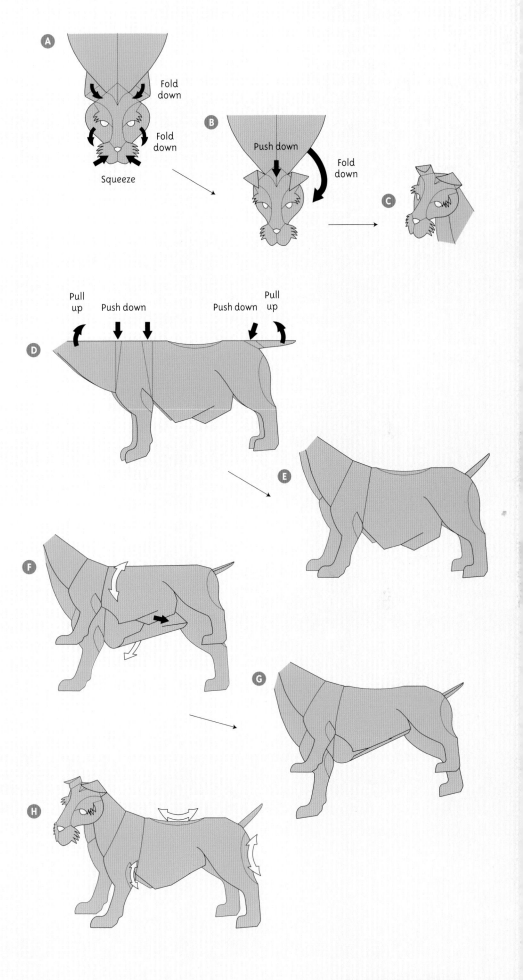

Mutt (puppy)

Having a heart of gold is far more important than having a fancy pedigree. Little Mutt pups, no matter their heritage, are often the best combinations of wiggly, cuddly, loveable company.

1 Using the Mutt (puppy) template on page 133, score the folding lines, then cut along all the solid lines, including the eyelids, the nose, and the tabs for the interlocking joints, as depicted in "How to Use This Book" on pages 7–13.

2 Pull up the eyelids. Fold up the muzzle toward the eyes. Fold down the ears Ⓐ.

3 Push up the cheeks and interlock the lower jaw joint by crossing the tabs Ⓑ.

4 Fold down the neck behind the head while you valley fold the top of the head Ⓒ Ⓓ.

5 Fold the body in half by following the scored centerline. Pocket fold the neck and the tail Ⓔ Ⓕ.

6 Round the body by rolling it over a dowel. Interlock the stomach joint by crossing the tabs Ⓖ Ⓗ.

TIP

One of the most charming qualities about a Mutt is that you're never quite sure of his pedigree(s)— the mystery is part of his allure. Feel free to personalize your Mutt Puppy and add whatever painted detail you wish.

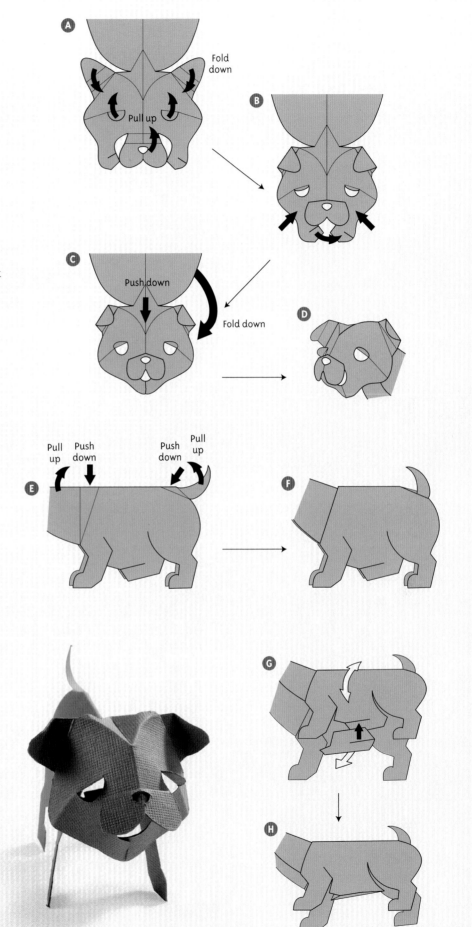

Yorkshire Terrier

Now here's a big personality in a petite package!
Yorkies are known for their fun, bold, and feisty
nature, despite the fact that they usually only weigh
between three and seven pounds.

BONUS PROJECT
available FREE at
www.larkcrafts.com/bonus

1 Using the Yorkshire Terrier template on page 142, score the folding lines, then cut along all the solid lines, including the openings of the eyes, the nose, and the tabs for the interlocking joint, as depicted in "How to Use This Book" on pages 7–13.

2 Push down the bases of the ears and fold them behind the head. Fold down the fur on the sides of the eyes. Push the muzzle back while squeezing in the cheeks **A**.

3 Fold down the neck behind the head while you valley fold the top of the head **B C**.

4 Fold the template in half by following the scored centerline **D**.

5 Fold the neck over the shoulders. Push down the top of the hips **E**.

6 Fold over the chest fur to the sides **F**.

7 Fold the front and hind legs following the scored lines and interlock the joint by crossing the tabs **G**.

8 Push down the head **H**.

9 Add color and pattern to your Yorkie by referencing the project photos.

TIP

When Yorkies are puppies, their fur is black and tan. As they mature, their fur becomes a lighter tan and steel blue color, and adult Yorkies are often groomed to have longer, luxurious coats. If you'd like to make a long-haired Yorkshire Terrier, visit www.larkcrafts.com/bonus for a downloadable template and how-to instructions.

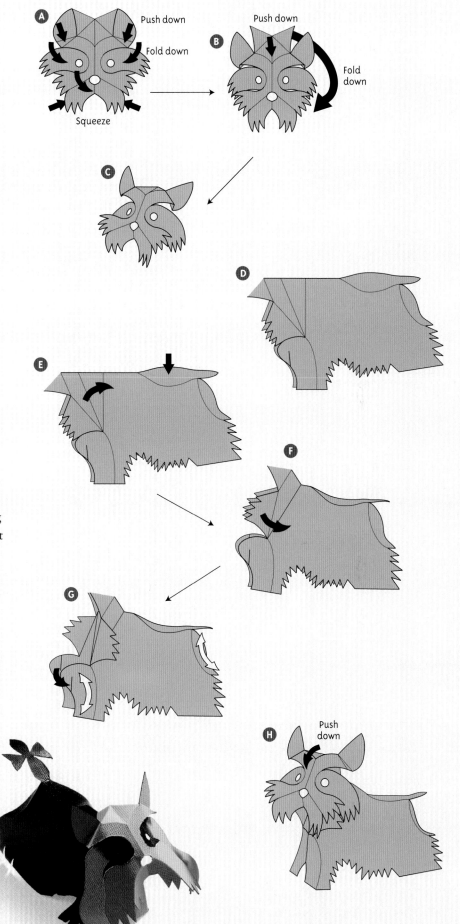

Great Dane

It's possible that the Great Dane is actually the world's biggest lap dog—these gentle giants are beloved for their sweet nature and affectionate temperament.

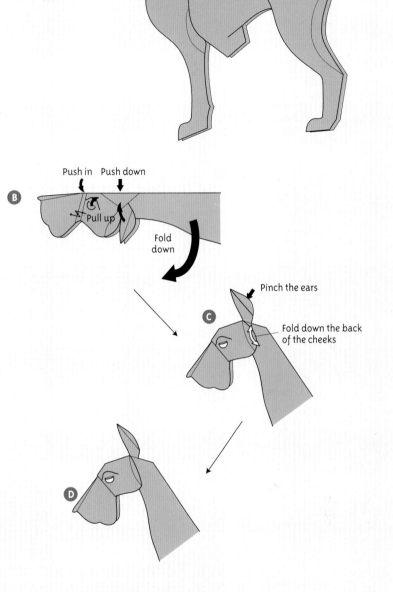

1 Using the Great Dane template on page 128, score the folding lines, then cut along all the solid lines, including the eyelids and the tabs for the interlocking joint, as depicted in "How to Use This Book" on pages 7–13.

2 Fold the template in half following the scored centerline Ⓐ.

3 Pull up the ears and the eyelids. Push up the muzzle and fold its top end under the eyes. Fold down the neck behind the head while you valley fold the top of the head Ⓑ.

4 Pinch and squeeze the ears. Fold the back of the cheeks Ⓒ Ⓓ.

5 Pocket fold the neck, the shoulders, and the tail Ⓔ Ⓕ.

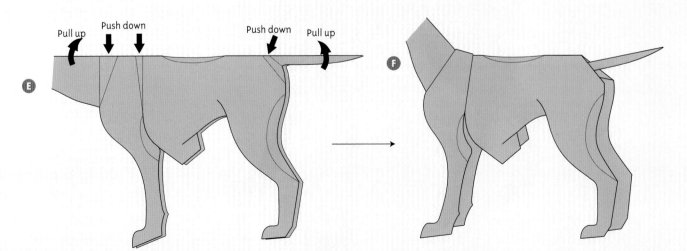

6 Round the body by rolling it over a dowel. Interlock the stomach joint by crossing the tabs **G**.

7 Add more curves to the back and the shoulders. Fold the front and the hind legs by following the scored lines **H**.

8 Add color and pattern to your Great Dane by referencing the project photos.

TIP
Want to make the Great Dane pictured with endearingly soft ears? Visit www.larkcrafts.com/bonus for a downloadable template and how-to instructions.

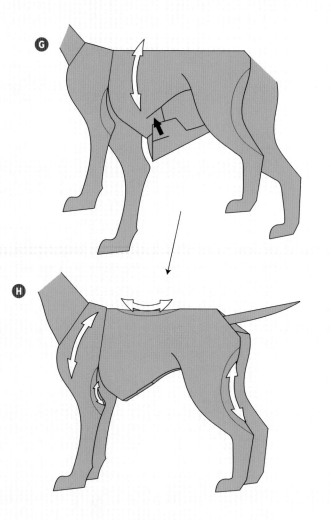

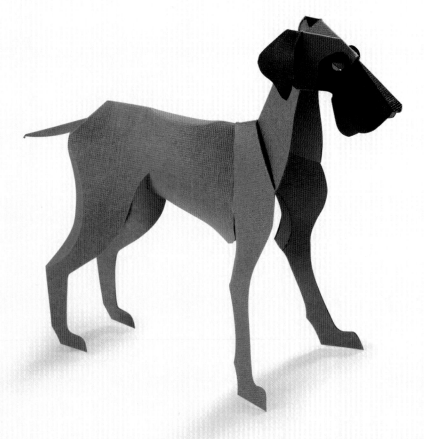

Bloodhound

The Bloodhound's loose skin around his head, neck, and face once earned him the affectionate description of a dog wearing a baggy suit. With a powerful sense of smell, Bloodhounds have long held a reputation as excellent trackers.

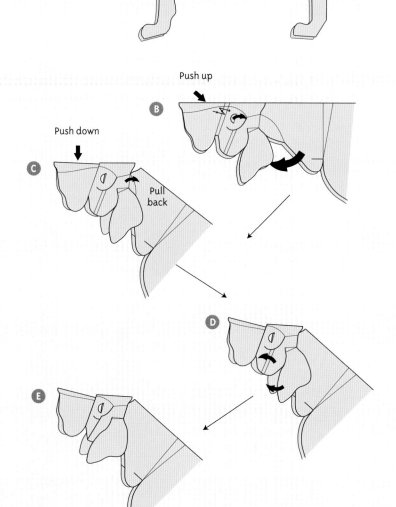

1 Using the Bloodhound template on page 112, score the folding lines, then cut along all the solid lines, including the eyelids and the tabs for the interlocking joints, as depicted in "How to Use This Book" on pages 7–13.

2 Fold the template in half following the scored centerline **A**.

3 Pull up the eyelids. Fold the neck in between the ears. Push up the muzzle and fold its top end under the eyes **B**.

4 Push down and flatten the bridge of the nose a little. Pull back the head over the top of the neck **C**.

5 Swing the ears to the front. Shape the folds of the cheeks following the scored lines **D** **E**.

6 Pocket fold the neck, the shoulders, and the tail **F** **G**.

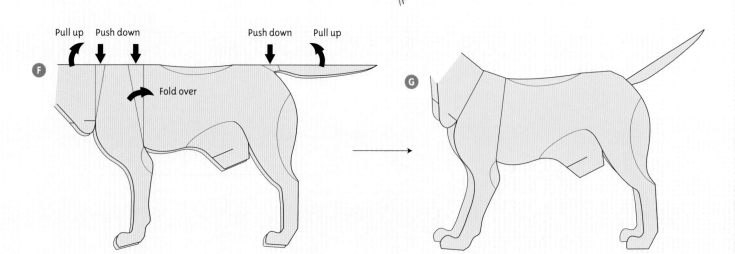

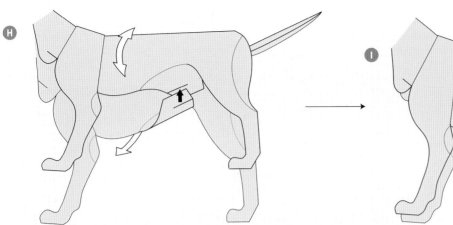

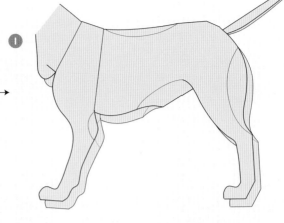

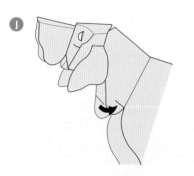

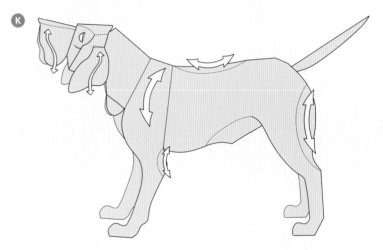

7 Round the body by rolling it over a dowel. Interlock the stomach joint by crossing the tabs **H** **I**.

8 Interlock the joint at the bottom of the neck **J**.

9 Add wavy curves to the droopy muzzle and ears. Push down the back to add more curve to it. Round the shoulders by rolling them over a dowel. Fold the front and hind legs following the scored lines **K**.

TIP
The Bloodhound featured in these project photos has a simple black nose and no other embellishment. Feel free to personalize your Bloodhound and add painted detail if you wish.

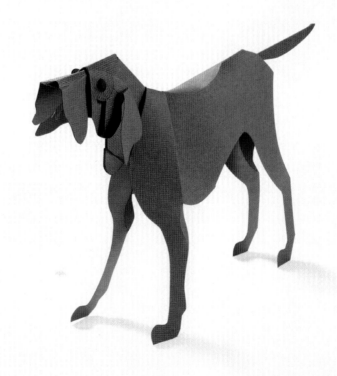

Basset Hound

Got a mystery? Put this pup on the case! A Basset Hound's long heavy body, short legs, droopy ears, and sweet disposition make him a pro when it comes to trailing a scent.

1 Using the Basset Hound template on page 109, score the folding lines, then cut along all the solid lines, including the eyelids and the tabs for the interlocking joint, as depicted in "How to Use This Book" on pages 7–13.

2 Fold the template in half by following the scored centerline Ⓐ.

3 Pull up the eyelids. Fold up the bases of the ears toward the head and swing the ears to the front. Shape the cheeks by following the scored lines. Open up the nose. Fold down the neck behind the head while you valley fold the top of the head Ⓑ Ⓒ.

4 Pocket fold the neck and the tail Ⓓ Ⓔ.

5 Round the body by rolling it over a dowel. Interlock the stomach joint by crossing the tabs Ⓕ Ⓖ.

6 Add more curve to the back by pushing it down. Fold the front and the hind legs by following the scored lines. Add wavy curves to the droopy ears and add more curves to the sides of the muzzle Ⓗ.

7 Add color and pattern to your Basset Hound by referencing the project photo. Want to turn your Basset Hound into a Sherlock Holmes? Make him a hunting hat and pipe with the instructions and template found on www.larkcrafts.com/bonus.

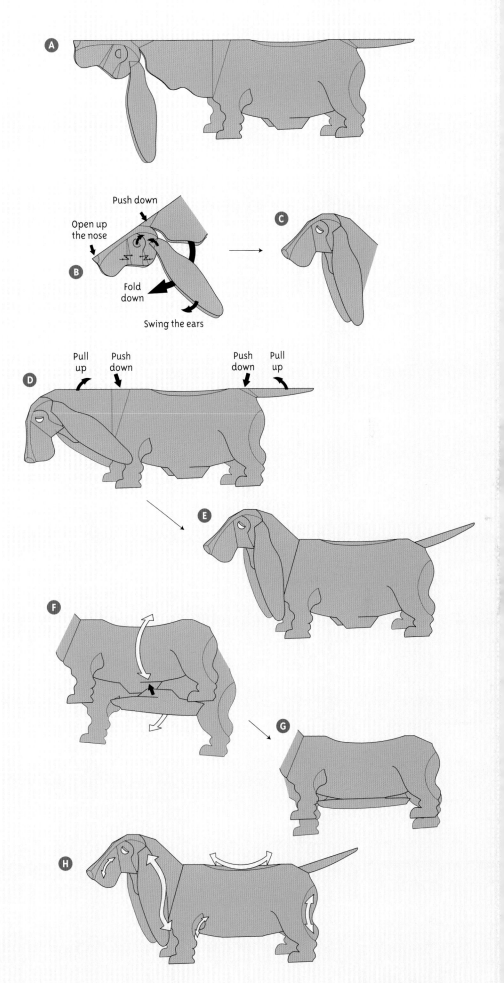

Boston Terrier

The Boston Terrier enjoys the nickname "the American Gentleman" because of his rather dapper appearance, gentle temperament, and companionable company.

1 Using the Boston Terrier template on page 113, score the folding lines, then cut along all the solid lines, including the eyelids, the nose, and the tabs for the interlocking joint, as depicted in "How to Use This Book" on pages 7–13.

2 Pull up the eyelids. Push down the bases of the ears and fold them behind the head. Pull up the muzzle toward the eyes Ⓐ.

3 Squeeze in the muzzle. Fold down the neck behind the head while you valley fold the top of the head Ⓑ.

4 Pinch and squeeze the ears Ⓒ.

5 Fold the body in half by following the scored centerline. Pull up the neck following the scored lines. Fold the shoulders over the back. Pocket fold the tail Ⓓ Ⓔ.

6 Round the body by rolling it over a dowel. Interlock the stomach joint by crossing the tabs Ⓕ Ⓖ.

7 Fold the front and the hind legs by following the scored lines Ⓗ.

8 Add color and pattern to your Boston Terrier by referencing the project photos.

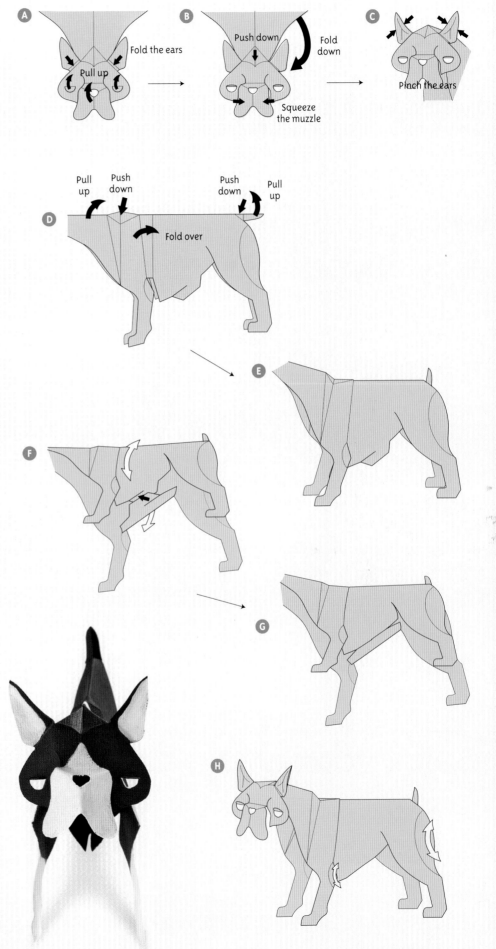

Chihuahua

Don't be fooled: the Chihuahua's teeny body is home to a mega-sized personality of sass, loyalty, confidence, and heart.

1 Using the Chihuahua template on page 116, score the folding lines, then cut along all the solid lines, including the eyelids and the tabs for the interlocking joint, as depicted in "How to Use This Book" on pages 7–13.

2 Fold the template in half by following the scored centerline **A**.

3 Pull up and push in the muzzle and fold its top end under the eyes. Fold down the neck behind the head while you valley fold the top of the head. Push down the bases of the ears. Fold them behind the head **B**.

4 Pinch and squeeze the ears. Push the face back to open it up a little. Pull up the eyelids. Push down the pocket of the nose, following the illustration **C D**.

5 Pocket fold the neck, the shoulders, and the tail. Pull up the hind legs over the stomach **E**.

6 Interlock the chest joint by crossing the tabs **F**.

7 Push the upper eyelids forward and pull back the cheeks. Fold the front and the hind legs by following the scored lines **G**.

8 Add color and pattern to your Chihuahua by referencing the project photos.

9 To keep this little Chihuahua from getting too cold in winter, make him a doggy sweater to stay warm and toasty! Look for the Chihuahua Sweater template and instructions on page 105.

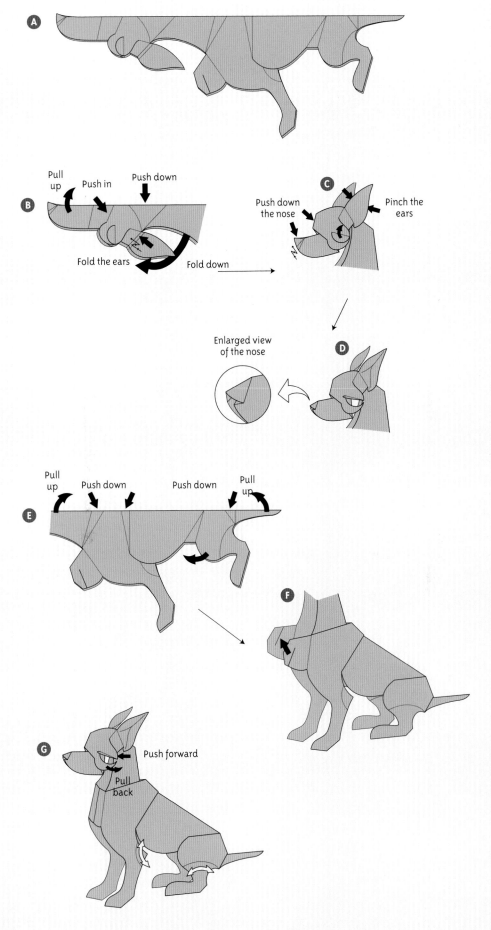

Cocker Spaniel

Pretty coats of glossy, flowing fur might make you think the Cocker Spaniel is all about looks, but think again: this sweet pal is up for adventure and good-natured play at every turn.

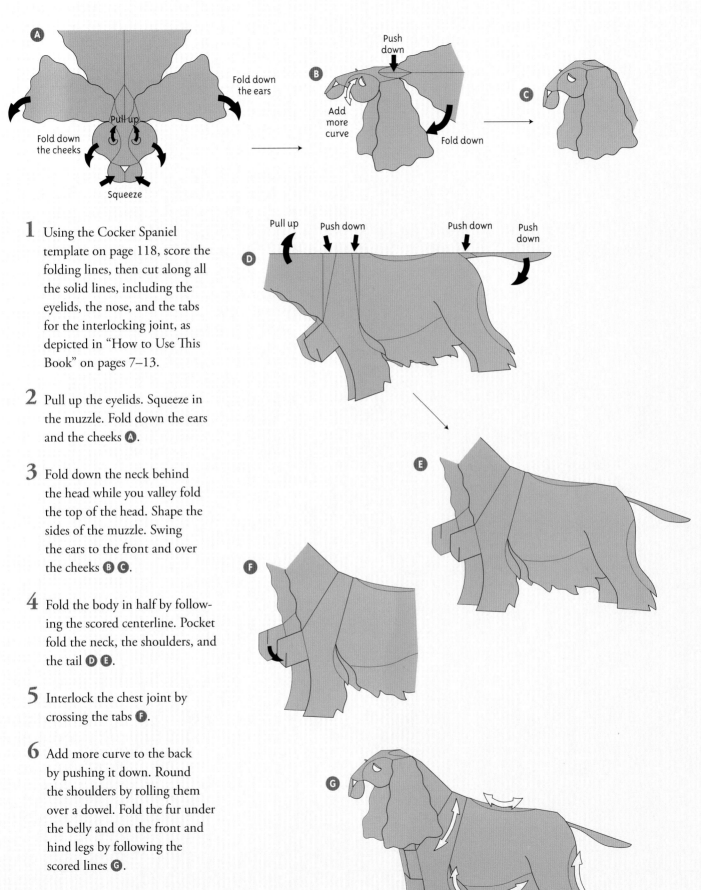

1 Using the Cocker Spaniel template on page 118, score the folding lines, then cut along all the solid lines, including the eyelids, the nose, and the tabs for the interlocking joint, as depicted in "How to Use This Book" on pages 7–13.

2 Pull up the eyelids. Squeeze in the muzzle. Fold down the ears and the cheeks **A**.

3 Fold down the neck behind the head while you valley fold the top of the head. Shape the sides of the muzzle. Swing the ears to the front and over the cheeks **B C**.

4 Fold the body in half by following the scored centerline. Pocket fold the neck, the shoulders, and the tail **D E**.

5 Interlock the chest joint by crossing the tabs **F**.

6 Add more curve to the back by pushing it down. Round the shoulders by rolling them over a dowel. Fold the fur under the belly and on the front and hind legs by following the scored lines **G**.

7 Add color and pattern to your Cocker Spaniel by referencing the project photo.

Corgi

The Corgi's low-to-the-ground body and natural herding tendencies have made it a valuable member of farms throughout history, and today the Corgi enjoys a reputation as a bright-eyed, sweet-mannered family companion.

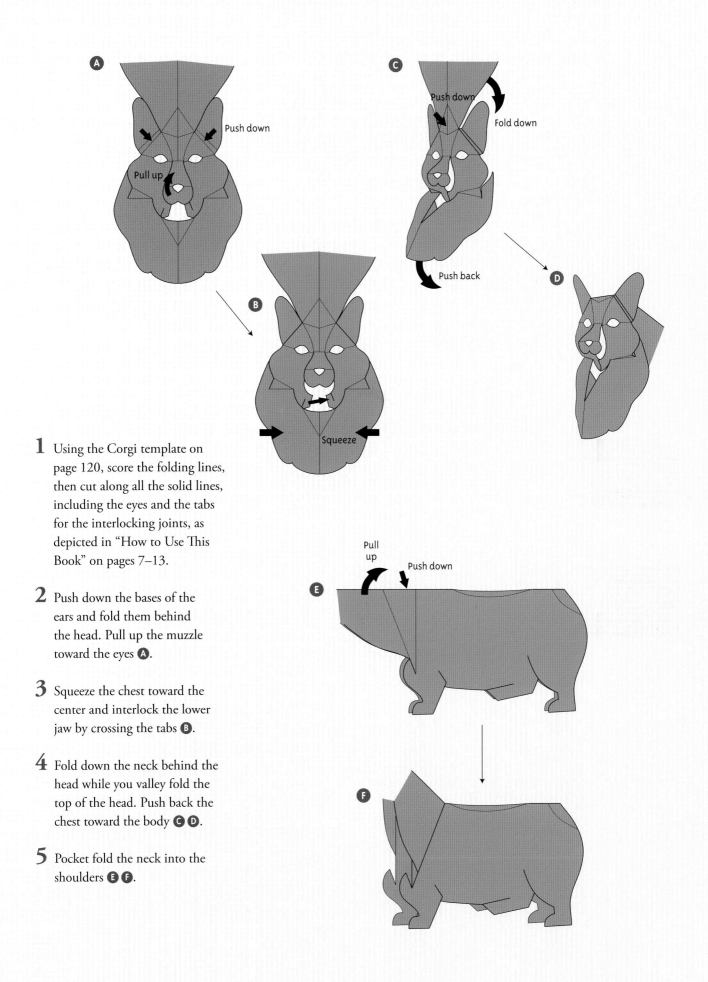

1 Using the Corgi template on page 120, score the folding lines, then cut along all the solid lines, including the eyes and the tabs for the interlocking joints, as depicted in "How to Use This Book" on pages 7–13.

2 Push down the bases of the ears and fold them behind the head. Pull up the muzzle toward the eyes Ⓐ.

3 Squeeze the chest toward the center and interlock the lower jaw by crossing the tabs Ⓑ.

4 Fold down the neck behind the head while you valley fold the top of the head. Push back the chest toward the body Ⓒ Ⓓ.

5 Pocket fold the neck into the shoulders Ⓔ Ⓕ.

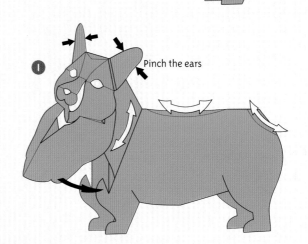

6 Round the body by rolling it over a dowel. Interlock the stomach joint by crossing the tabs **G** **H**.

7 Pinch and squeeze the ears. Lower the head and interlock the notches at the bottom of the chest with the cuts made in the front legs. Add more curve to the neck and the back. Push in the top of the hips following the scored lines **I**.

8 Add color and pattern to your Corgi by referencing the project photos.

Pinch the ears

English Bulldog

Talk about heart! The English Bulldog is a wrinkly, snuffly, stout barrel of affection and gentleness whose bad-boy exterior belies a mellow, friendly character.

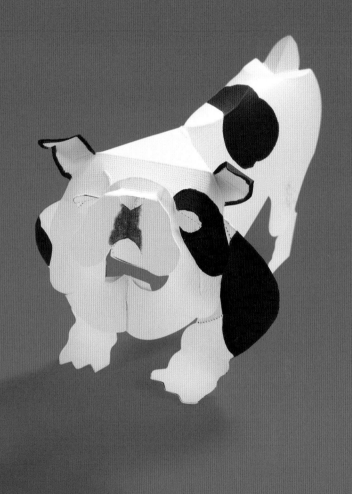

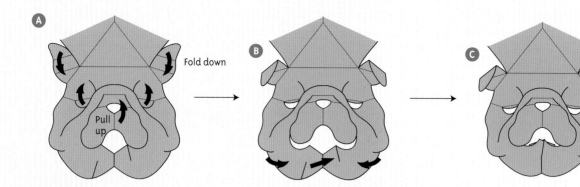

1 Using the English Bulldog template on page 124, score the folding lines, then cut along all the solid lines, including the eyelids, the nose, the mouth, and the tabs for the interlocking joints, as depicted in "How to Use This Book" on pages 7–13.

2 Pull up the eyelids. Fold down the ears. Pull up the muzzle toward the eyes **A**.

3 Bring the two halves of the lower jaw together and interlock the joint by crossing the tabs **B** **C**.

4 Fold the body in half by following the scored centerline. Pull up the neck over the shoulders. Pocket fold the tail into the hips **D** **E**.

F

G

H

Fold
down

Fold out

I

J

5 Round the body by rolling it over a dowel. Interlock the stomach joint by crossing the tabs **F** **G**.

6 Fold down the head. Fold out the font legs from the shoulder lines **H**.

7 Add more curve to the back by pushing it down. Round the upper front legs by following the scored lines **I**.

8 Roll up the paws of the front legs **I**.

9 Add color and pattern to your English Bulldog by referencing the project photos.

TIP

Let your tenderhearted English Bulldog pretend to be a tough guy: make him a spike-studded collar using the template on page 105.

French Bulldog

With endearing bat-like ears and a compact little body, the French Bulldog is friendly, affectionate, and loves people. His sweet cuteness helps balance out his tendency to snore like a freight train!

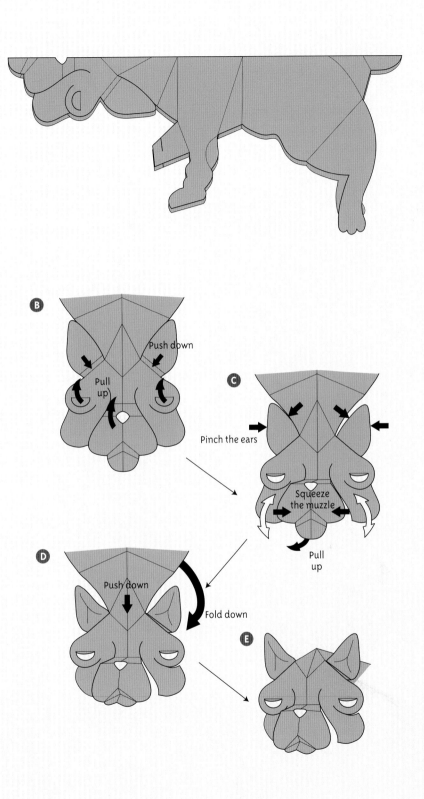

1 Using the French Bulldog template on page 125, score the folding lines, then cut along all the solid lines, including the eyelids, the nose, and the tabs for the interlocking joint, as depicted in "How to Use This Book" on pages 7–13.

2 Fold the template in half by following the scored centerline Ⓐ.

3 Push down the bases of the ears and fold them behind the head. Pull up the eyelids. Pull up the muzzle toward the eyes Ⓑ.

4 Squeeze the ears and the muzzle. Round the cheeks by rolling them over a dowel. Then pull up the tongue forward by pocket folding it Ⓒ.

5 Fold down the neck behind the head while you valley fold the top of the head Ⓓ Ⓔ.

6 Push down the neck into the shoulders. Pull up the shoulders over the stomach. Pocket fold the tail into the hips **F G**.

7 Interlock the chest joint by crossing the tabs. Fold the front legs by following the scored lines **H**.

8 Fold over both legs to the right side of the body **I J K**.

9 Add color and pattern to your French Bulldog by referencing the project photos.

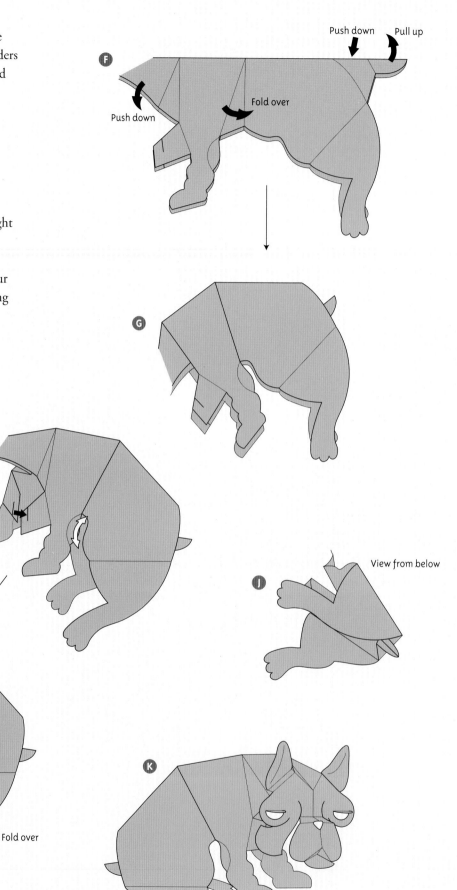

Greyhound

Superman's "faster than a speeding bullet" tagline has met its match: the Greyhound is primarily known for her incredible speed and athleticism, though she's just as beloved for her gentle and sensitive nature.

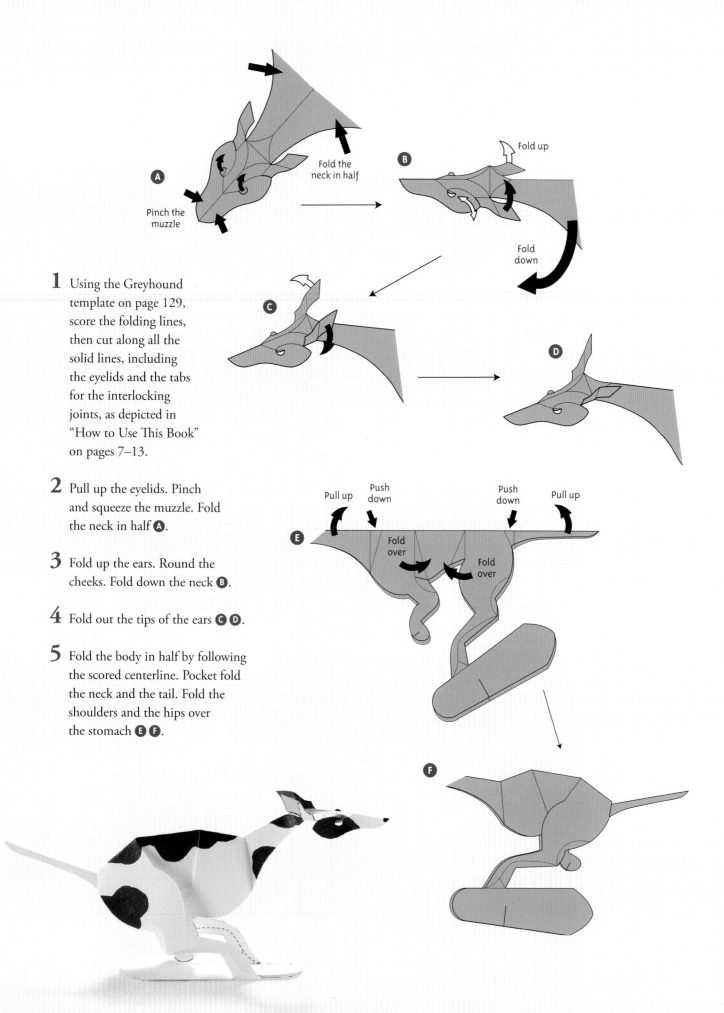

1 Using the Greyhound template on page 129, score the folding lines, then cut along all the solid lines, including the eyelids and the tabs for the interlocking joints, as depicted in "How to Use This Book" on pages 7–13.

2 Pull up the eyelids. Pinch and squeeze the muzzle. Fold the neck in half **A**.

3 Fold up the ears. Round the cheeks. Fold down the neck **B**.

4 Fold out the tips of the ears **C D**.

5 Fold the body in half by following the scored centerline. Pocket fold the neck and the tail. Fold the shoulders and the hips over the stomach **E F**.

6 Interlock the front leg paws by crossing the tabs **G** **H**.

7 Interlock the two bases by crossing the cut lines in them **I** **J**.

8 Fold the scored lines of the hind legs. Squeeze the paws to add more strength to them **K**.

9 Fold the front legs by following the scored lines **L**.

10 Adjust the angle of the legs to make the dog stand up on the ground **M**.

11 Add color and pattern to your Greyhound by referencing the project photos.

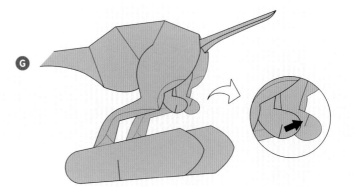

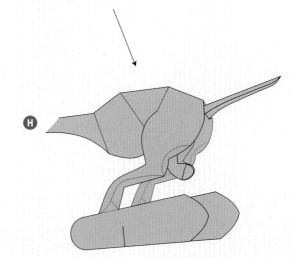

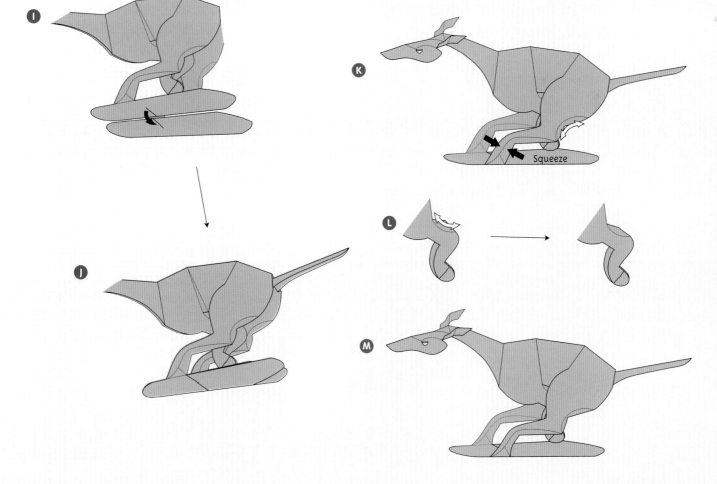

Golden Retriever

In addition to being one of the best-loved dogs in the U.S., the Golden Retriever is also a well-known hunting companion, guide and assistant dog, and valuable search and rescue dog.

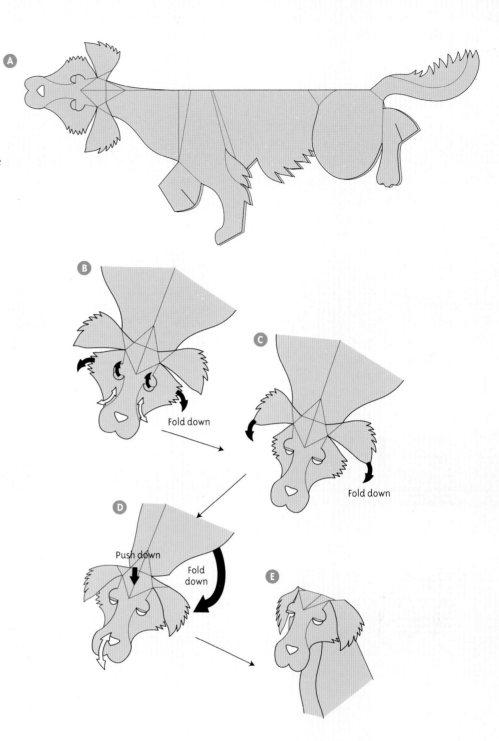

1 Using the Golden Retriever template on page 127, score the folding lines, then cut along all the solid lines, including the eyelids, the nose, and the tabs for the interlocking joints, as depicted in "How to Use This Book" on pages 7–13.

2 Fold the template in half by following the scored centerline except for the face and the tail **A**.

3 Pull up the eyelids. Fold down the cheeks. Add curves to both sides of the muzzle **B**.

4 Fold down and swing the ears over the cheeks **C**.

5 Fold down the neck behind the head while you valley fold the top of the head. Round the muzzle by rolling it over a dowel **D E**.

6 Pocket fold the neck into the shoulders. Pull the shoulders and the hind legs over the stomach **F G**.

Fold down

Fold down

Push down

Fold down

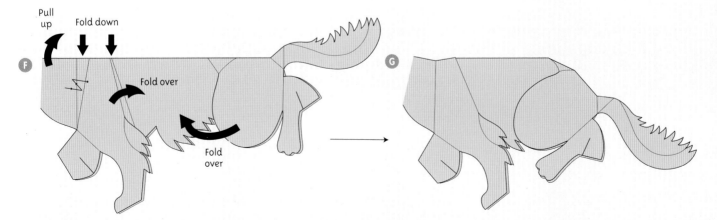

Pull up

Fold down

Fold over

Fold over

7   Interlock the chest joint by crossing the tabs **H I**.

8   Interlock the hind leg joint by crossing the tabs located on the underside of the legs **J K**.

9   Swing up the tail, following the scored folding line at its base **L**.

10 Fold the front legs by following the scored lines. Add more curve to the tail **M**.

11 The Golden Retriever featured in these project photos has no added color or embellishment, but feel free to personalize your pup and add painted detail if you wish.

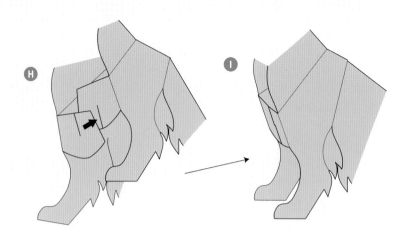

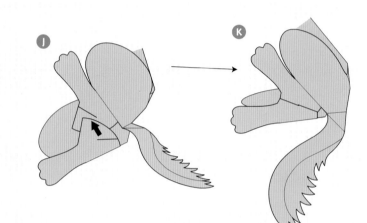

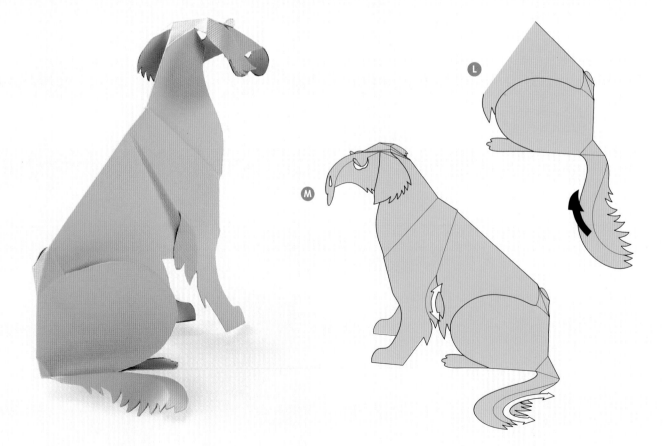

Labrador Retriever

Over the river and through the woods, Labrador Retrievers are fun-loving adventure pups: eager to play, gentle at heart, and often beloved family pets.

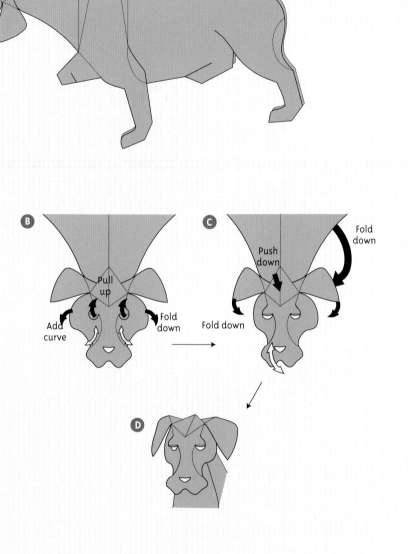

1 Using the Labrador Retriever template on page 131, score the folding lines, then cut along all the solid lines, including the eyelids, the nose, and the tabs for the interlocking joints, as depicted in "How to Use This Book" on pages 7–13.

2 Fold the body in half by following the scored centerline **A**.

3 Pull up the eyelids. Fold down the cheeks, and add curves to the sides of the muzzle **B**.

4 Fold down the ears. Round the muzzle by rolling it over a dowel. Fold down the neck behind the head while you valley fold the top of the head **C D**.

5 Pocket fold the neck, the shoulders, and the tail **E F**.

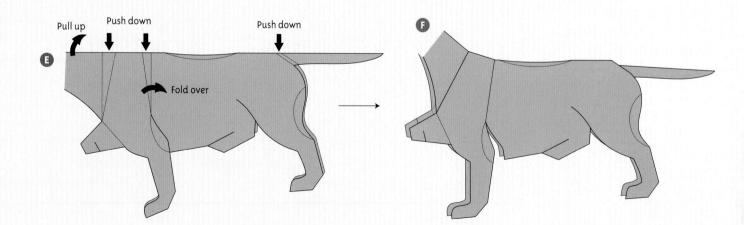

G

H

I

J

6 Round the body by rolling it over a dowel. Interlock the stomach joint by crossing the tabs **G** **H**.

7 Interlock the chest joint next by crossing the tabs **I**.

8 Add more curve to the back by pushing it down. Round the shoulders by rolling them over a dowel. Fold the front and hind legs by following the scored lines **J**.

TIP

Yellow Labs, Black Labs, and Chocolate Labs are as easy as one, two, three, when you print the template on paper in coordinating colors. The Labs featured in these project photos have no added color or embellishment, but feel free to personalize your Labrador Retriever and add painted detail if you wish.

Mutt (adult)

Love is the best pedigree any dog could have! Whether she's big or small, scruffy or sleek, silly or sophisticated, a Mutt's "multi-flavor" background simply adds to her winning charm.

1. Using the Mutt (adult) template on page 132, score the folding lines, then cut along all the solid lines, including the eyes, the nose, and the tabs for the interlocking joint, as depicted in "How to Use This Book" on pages 7–13.

2. Fold down the ears a little toward the face. Fold down the cheeks, then the beard Ⓐ.

3. Fold down the neck behind the head while you valley fold the top of the head Ⓑ Ⓒ.

4. Fold the body in half by following the scored centerline. Pocket fold the neck, the shoulders, and the tail Ⓓ Ⓔ.

5. Round the body by rolling it over a dowel. Interlock the stomach joint by crossing the tabs Ⓕ Ⓖ.

6. Add more curve to the back by pushing it down. Round the shoulders by rolling them over a dowel. Curl the tail. Fold the front and hind legs by following the scored lines Ⓗ.

TIP

No two dogs look the same, and Mutts surely come in all shapes and sizes! Add color and pattern to your Mutt by referencing the project photo, or celebrate your pup's unique appearance by personalizing her look with individual color and embellishment.

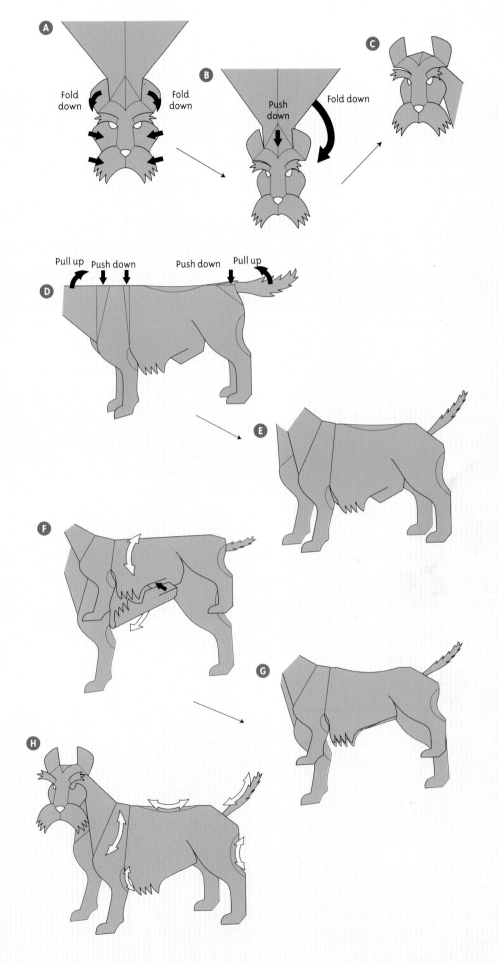

Pomeranian

Now a toy breed typically weighing only three to seven pounds, the Pomeranian was once a larger breed, weighing nearly 30 pounds and commonly herding sheep. Maybe that's why this little fluff of a pup has such a big personality!

1 Using the Pomeranian template on page 134, score the folding lines, then cut along all the solid lines, including the nose and the tabs for the interlocking joint, as depicted in "How to Use This Book" on pages 7–13.

2 Push down the bases of the ears. Fold them behind the head. Pull the two halves of the chest together **A**.

3 Interlock the chest joint by crossing the tabs. Pull up the tongue. Fold down the neck behind the head while you valley fold the top of the head **B**.

4 Fold back the muzzle. Shape the chest by rolling it over a dowel **C**.

5 Fold the body in half by following the scored centerline. Pocket fold the neck into the shoulders. Pull up the hips over the back **D** **E**.

6 Lower the head and interlock the notches at the bottom of the chest with the cuts made in the front legs **F** **G**.

7 Push the base of the tail into the hips **H** **I**.

8 Fold the tail over the hips. Shape the tail by rolling it over a dowel **J**.

9 Add color and pattern to your Pomeranian by referencing the project photo.

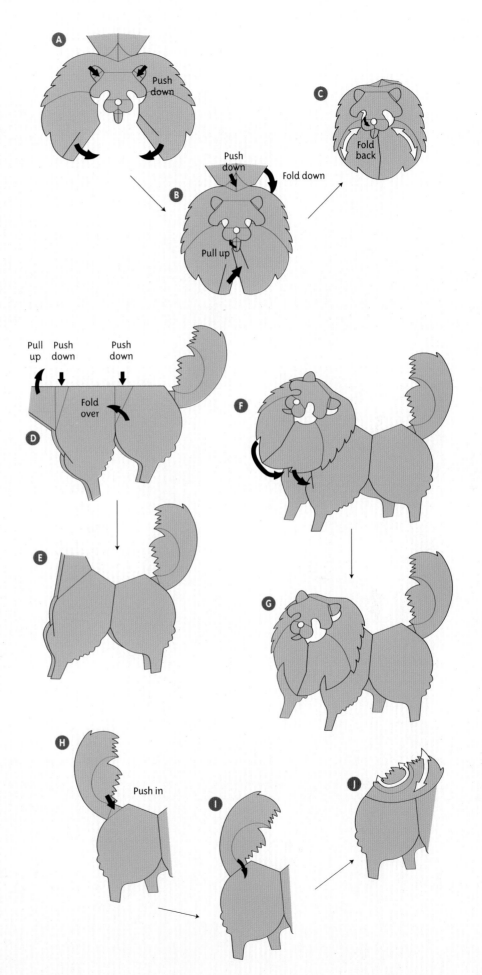

Siberian Husky

With a pedigree rooted in Northeast Asia, the quick-footed, adventurous Siberian Husky is often a sled dog, happiest in cool climates, and always ready for an escapade.

1 Using the Siberian Husky template on page 140, score the folding lines, then cut along all the solid lines, including the eyes, the nose, the mouth, and the tabs for the interlocking joint, as depicted in "How to Use This Book" on pages 7–13.

2 Push down the bases of the ears. Fold them behind the head. Pull up the muzzle toward the eyes. Push in the eyes with a sharp tool such as the tip of an awl Ⓐ.

3 Squeeze in the outside edges of the lower jaw, push in the center of the chest, and interlock the two halves of the jaw together by crossing the cut lines Ⓑ.

4 Fold down the neck behind the head while you valley fold the top of the head Ⓒ Ⓓ.

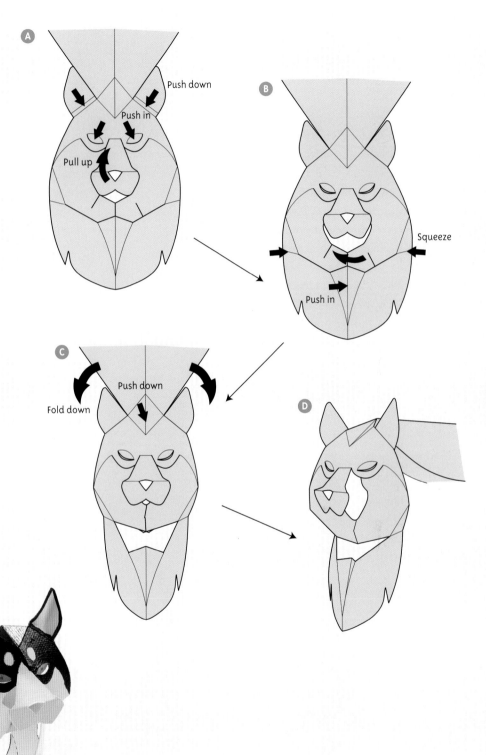

Ⓐ Push down Push in Pull up

Ⓑ Squeeze Push in

Ⓒ Fold down Push down

Ⓓ

5 Fold the body in half by following the scored centerline. Pocket fold the neck and the shoulders. Pull up the tail. Push the base of the tail into the hips **E F**.

6 Round the body by rolling it over a dowel. Interlock the chest joint by crossing the tabs **G H**.

7 Lower the head and interlock the notches at the bottom of the chest with the cuts made in the front legs. Add more curve to the back by pushing it down. Round the shoulders by rolling them over a dowel. Fold the front and the hind legs by following the scored lines. Shape the tail **I J**.

TIP

Add color and pattern to your Siberian Husky by referencing the project photos. Huskies are well known for having piercing blue eyes: paint the eyes in light blue with a small brush and create pupils by adding tiny black dots in the center.

Pug

One look at a Pug's smiley face, wagging curly tail, and alert little countenance will have you smiling and wagging, too! These comical, loving fellows are excellent companions.

1 Using the Pug template on page 136, score the folding lines, then cut along all the solid lines, including the eyelids, the nose, the mouth, and the tabs for the interlocking joints, as depicted in "How to Use This Book" on pages 7–13.

2 Pull the two halves of the lower jaw together and interlock the joint by crossing the tabs Ⓐ.

3 Squeeze and valley fold the center of the muzzle. Pull out the circles around the eyes Ⓑ.

4 Pull up the eyelids. Fold down the ears Ⓒ Ⓓ.

5 Pocket fold the neck and the shoulders. Push down the base of the tail. Round the body by rolling it over a dowel Ⓔ Ⓕ.

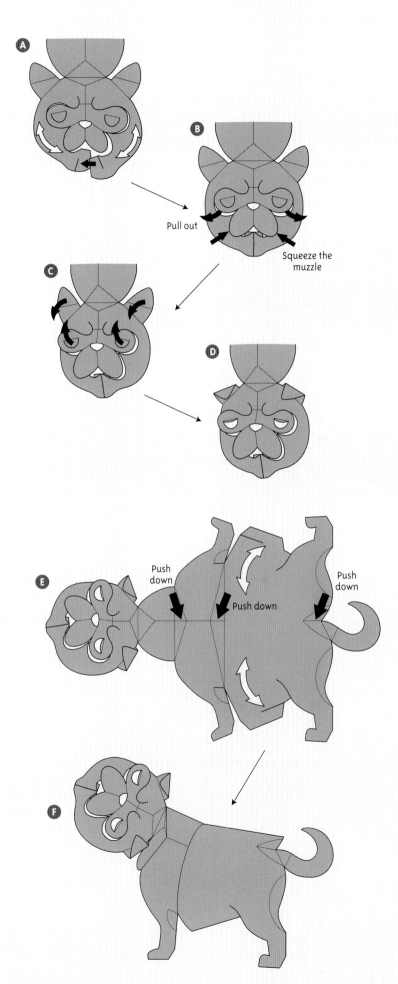

6 Interlock the stomach joint by crossing the tabs **G**.

7 Fold the tail over. Fold the front and the hind legs by following the scored lines **H** **I**.

8 Pull down the head **J** **K**.

9 Add color and pattern to your Pug by referencing the project photos, or simply use black paper to make a black Pug.

Pull down

Chinese Crested

The Hairless Chinese Crested is instantly recognizable by the crest of hair on his head, the plume of hair on his tail, and the "socks" of hair on his feet. This petite breed pairs his distinctive appearance with a sweet, cuddly, and bright demeanor.

1 Using the Chinese Crested template on page 117, score the folding lines, then cut along all the solid lines, including the eyelids, the hair, and the tabs for the interlocking joint, as depicted in "How to Use This Book" on pages 7–13.

2 Fold the template in half by following the scored centerline **A**.

3 Push up the muzzle and fold its top end under the eyes. Fold down the neck behind the head while you valley fold the top of the head **B**.

4 Pull up the eyelids. Push the tongue up and fold it under the chin **C**.

5 Raise the chin and fold down the hair on the head over the eyes **D E**.

6 Pocket fold the neck and the tail. Pull the shoulders and the hips over the stomach **F G**.

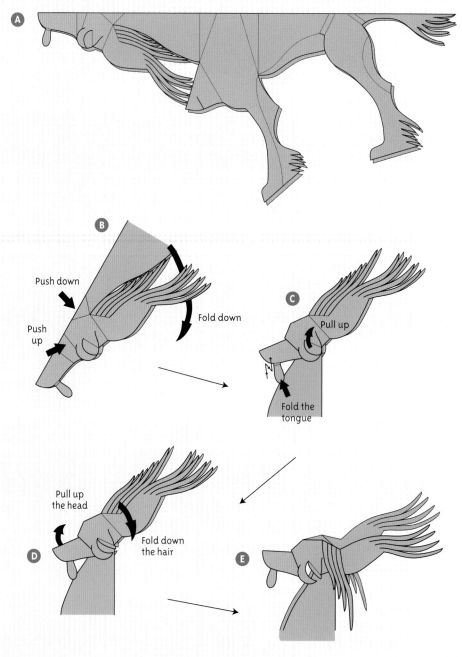

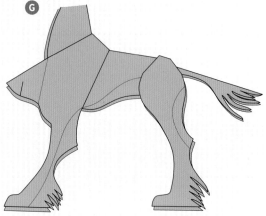

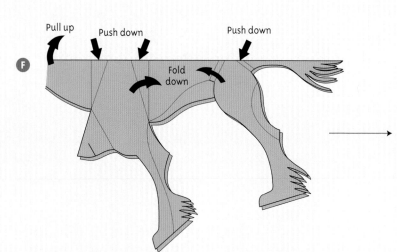

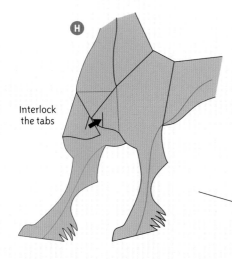

Interlock
the tabs

7 Interlock the chest joint by crossing the tabs. Fold the front legs by following the scored lines **H I**.

8 Shape the legs and the stomach by following the scored lines. Add wavy curves to the hair on the ears and to the hair on the head **J**.

9 Add color and pattern to your Chinese Crested by referencing the project photos.

Pull down

Round the ears

Poodle

The Poodle, while often stereotyped as a fussy, fluffy breed, is really a phenomenally smart, agile, and active dog. With such great intelligence, it just goes to show that you can't judge a (pretty) book entirely by its cover.

1 Using the Poodle template on page 135, score the folding lines, then cut along all the solid lines, including the eyelids and the cuts for the interlocking joint, as depicted in "How to Use This Book" on pages 7–13.

2 Pull up the eyelids. Fold down the ears. Squeeze in the chest **A**.

3 Pull up the forehead and push it back toward the head. Round the head by rolling it over a dowel. Pinch and squeeze the nose to make it pointed **B C**.

4 Pull up the neck and fold it over the shoulders. Pocket fold the shoulders over the back, and pull up the tail and fold it into the hips **D**.

5 Push down the back to add more curve to it. Fold the hind legs following the scored lines. Fold up the stomach **E F**.

6 Pull down the head. Interlock the notches at the bottom of the chest with the cuts made in the front legs **G**.

7 The Poodles featured in these project photos have simple black noses without any additional painted pattern. Simply change the paper color to reflect the many coat colors among the Poodle breed: white, silver, black, blue, brown, café au lait, cream, apricot, gray, red, and even brindle.

8 Give your highly intelligent Poodle something to wag about: make her a jacket! Find the Poodle Jacket template and instructions on page 104.

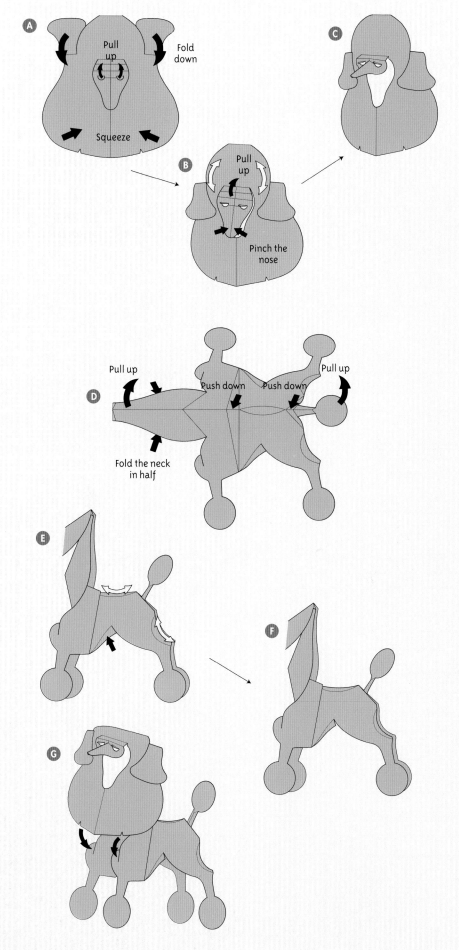

Shar-Pei

Don't let these droopy folds and walrus-like muzzle
fool you: the Shar-Pei, which means "sandy coat,"
is a dignified fellow, known for his gentle calmness
and devotion to family.

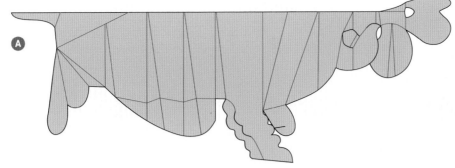

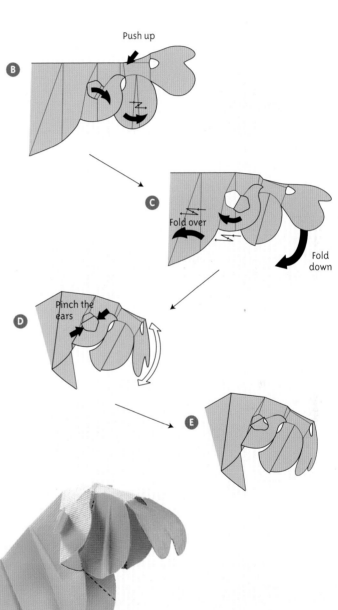

1 Using the Shar-Pei template on page 138, score the folding lines, then cut along all the solid lines, including the eyes, the ears, the nose, and the tabs for the interlocking joint, as depicted in "How to Use This Book" on pages 7–13.

2 Fold the template in half by following the scored centerline. Leave the muzzle unfolded **A**.

3 Fold down the ears. Shape the folds of the cheeks by following the scored lines. Push up the muzzle toward the forehead **B**.

4 Fold down the muzzle. Shape the folds of the head and the neck by following the scored lines **C**.

5 Pinch and squeeze the ears. Round the muzzle by rolling it over a dowel **D** **E**.

6 Pull the back of the neck over the shoulders. Pocket fold the tail into the hips **F**.

7 Work on the folds of the torso next **G**.

8 Push up the hind legs into the hips. Fold in the bottom of the bunched-up torso to hold the wrinkles of the torso **H**.

9 Fold the shoulders over the torso. Fold the hind legs out to the sides so that your Shar-Pei will sit comfortably on the ground. Fold the front legs **I**.

10 Interlock the chest joint by crossing the tabs **J K**.

TIP

The Shar-Pei featured in these project photos has a simple tan muzzle and no other embellishment, but feel free to personalize your pup and add painted detail if you wish.

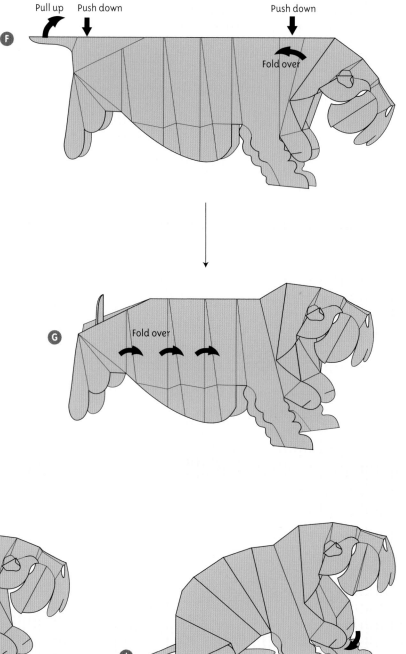

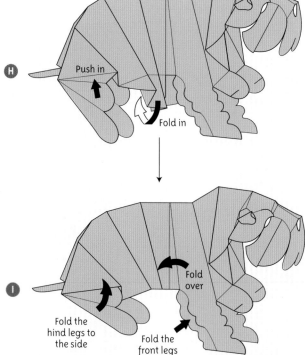

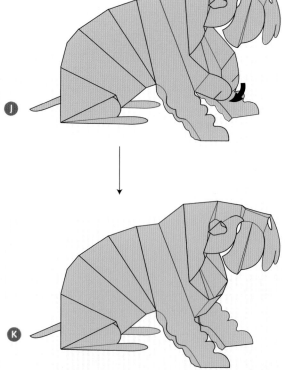

Shih Tzu

The word Shih Tzu actually means "lion," which befits this noble-looking pup: as a companion dog throughout history, the Shih Tzu was the cherished palace pet of Chinese royals during the Ming Dynasty.

1 Using the Shih Tzu template on page 139, score the folding lines, then cut along all the solid lines, including the eyes, the nose, the mouth, the curved lines in the fur, and the tabs for the interlocking joints, as depicted in "How to Use This Book" on pages 7–13.

2 Fold down the ears and round both sides of the head by rolling them over a dowel. Fold down the fur on the sides of the eyes. Then pull up the muzzle toward the eyes **A**.

3 Bring both sides of the cheeks together and interlock the joint in the middle by crossing the tabs **B**.

4 Fold down the neck behind the head while you valley fold the top of the head **C**.

5 Add wavy curves to the ears by rolling them over a dowel. Push the chin back toward the neck **D**.

6 Fold the body in half by following the scored centerline. Pocket fold the neck over the shoulders, then fold the shoulders over the back **E**.

7 Add curves to the hips by following the scored lines **F**.

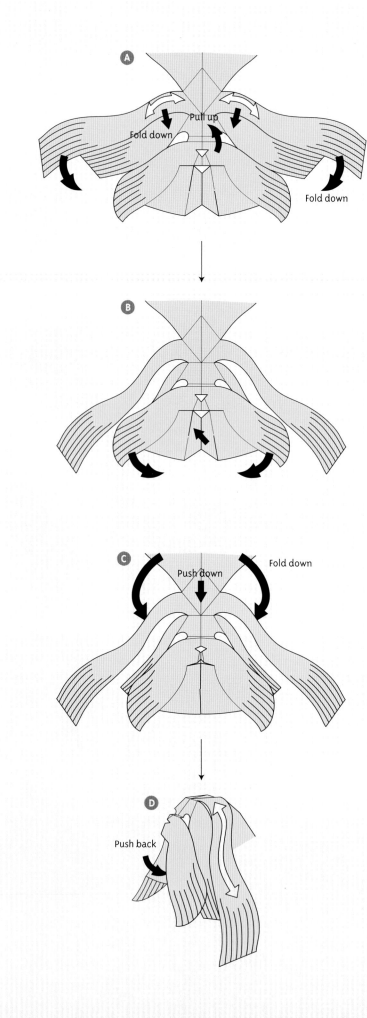

8 Interlock the hip joint by crossing the tabs **G** **H**.

9 Add more curve to the back by pushing it down. Fold down the tail over the hips **I**.

10 Add wavy curves to the tail by rolling it over a dowel **J**.

11 Add color and pattern to your Shih Tzu by referencing the project photos.

12 If you want to give your Shih Tzu a sweet little bow, use the template and instructions for the Shih Tzu Bow on page 103. Make a small cut in the top of the dog's head and insert the bow's pointed tip into the cut.

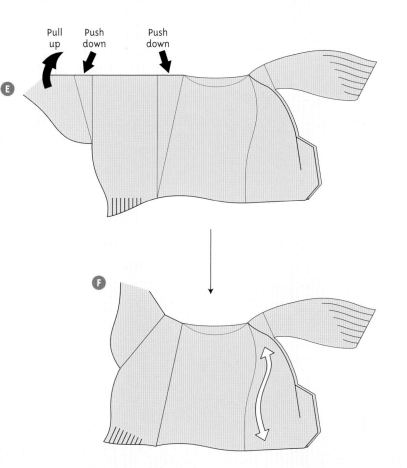

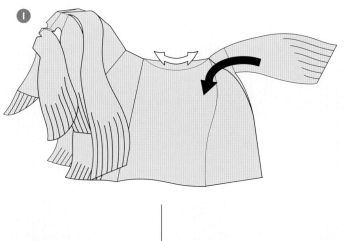

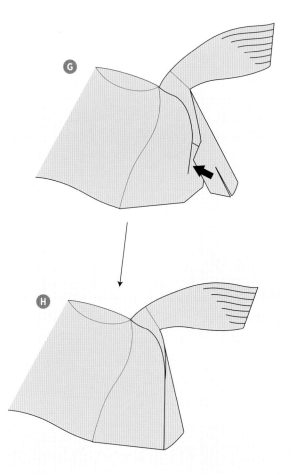

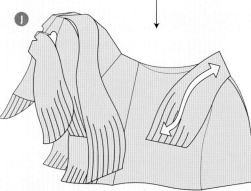

Best in Show Ribbon

1 Copy the template of the ribbon onto a sheet of cardstock paper.

2 Score the dotted lines.

3 Cut out the template along the solid lines including two small cuts in the center of the rosette.

4 Fold the template following the scored dotted lines.

5 Insert the tab of the ribbon into one of the cuts of the rosette as described in the illustration.

6 Fold down the tab and insert its end into the other cut.

7 To add the texture, draw the lines on the rosette with a scoring tool starting from the center and moving toward the edge.

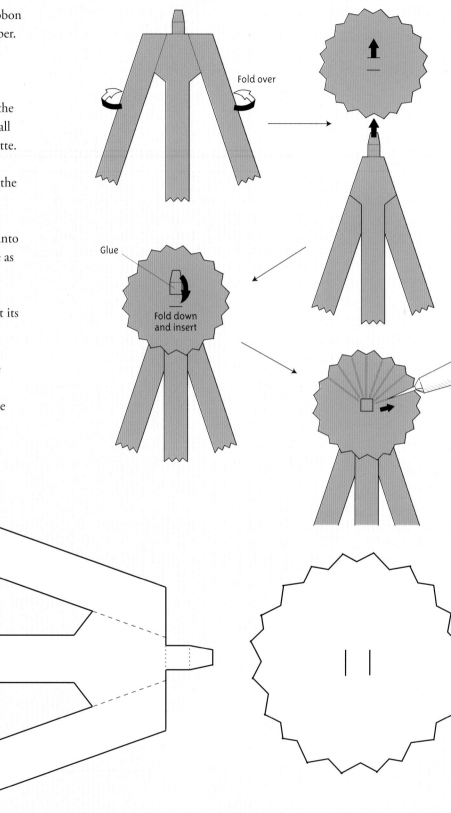

Shih Tzu Bow

1 Copy the template of the bow onto a sheet of cardstock paper.

2 Score the dotted lines.

3 Cut out the template along the solid lines including the ones inside the fur.

4 Fold the template following the scored dotted lines.

5 Add a curve to the fur with a dowel.

6 Make a small cut at the top of the head of your Shih Tzu with a craft knife.

7 Insert the pointed tip of the bow into the cut.

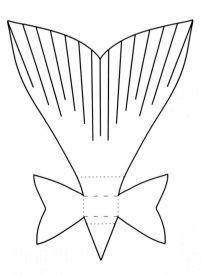

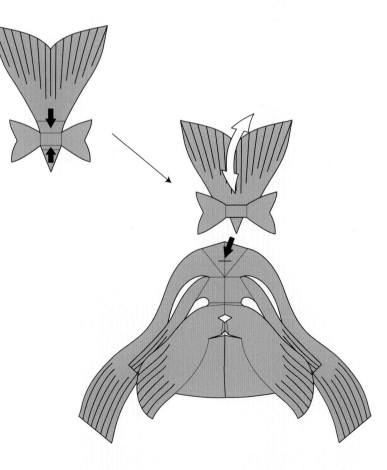

Poodle Jacket

1 Copy the template of the jacket onto a sheet of cardstock paper.

2 Score the dotted lines.

3 Cut out the template along the solid lines including the circles.

4 Fold the template following the scored dotted lines. Place the jacket right on the back of your poodle.

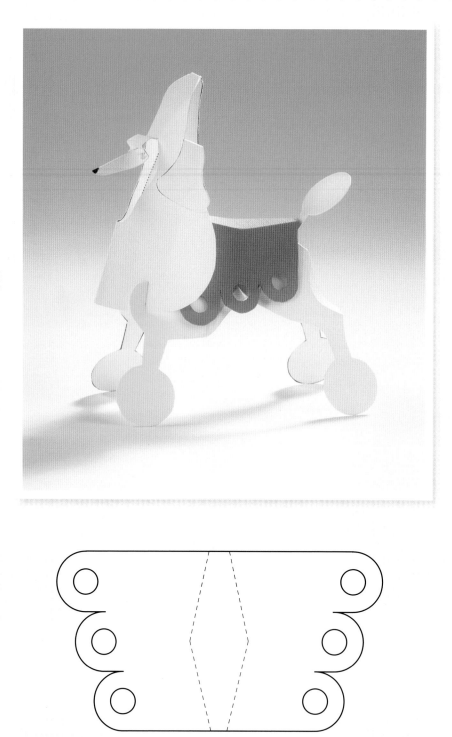

Sweater for Chihuahua

1 Copy the template onto a sheet of cardstock paper.

2 Score along the dotted folded lines.

3 Cut the template out along the solid lines.

4 Fold the template following the dotted lines.

5 Put the sweater on your Chihuahua.

6 Interlock the tabs of the chest joint.

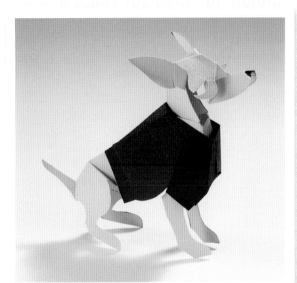

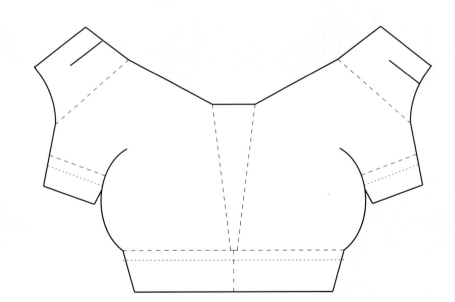

Dog Collars

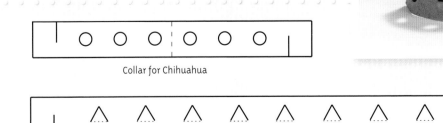

Collar for Chihuahua

Spike Studded Collar for English Bulldog

Dog House

1 Copy the template onto a sheet of cardstock paper. You can make your dog house size-appropriate for your dog.

2 Score dotted folding lines.

3 Cut the template out along the solid lines.

4 Fold the template following the dotted lines.

5 Fold the bone-shaped name plate and insert its pointed tip into the slit.

6 Interlock the tabs of the joint.

7 Apply glue to 2 tabs where indicated.

8 Glue the roof down to the dog house.

9 Write the name of your dog on the name plate.

Roof

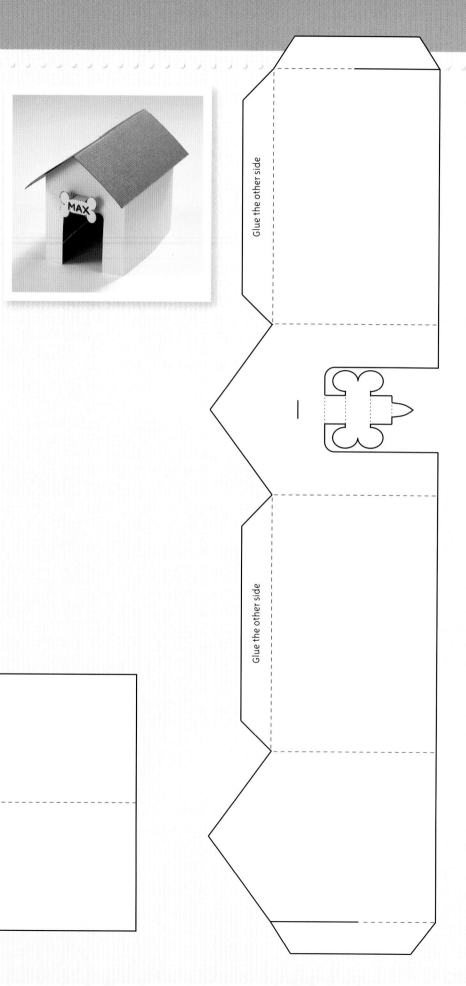

Glue the other side

Glue the other side

Fire Hydrant

1 Copy the template onto a sheet of cardstock paper.

2 Score along the dotted folding lines.

3 Cut the template out along the solid lines.

4 Fold the template following the dotted lines.

5 Interlock the tabs of the joint at the bottom.

6 Round the 2 hose connectors on the sides.

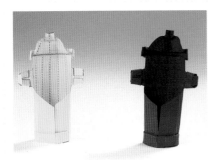

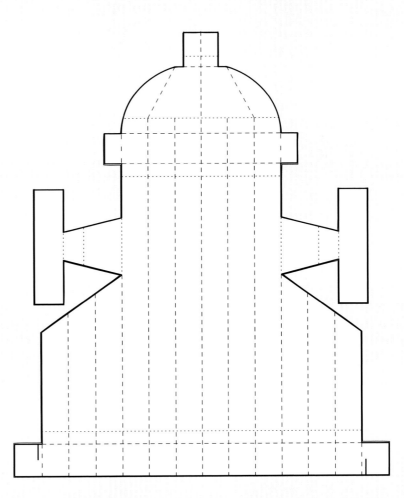

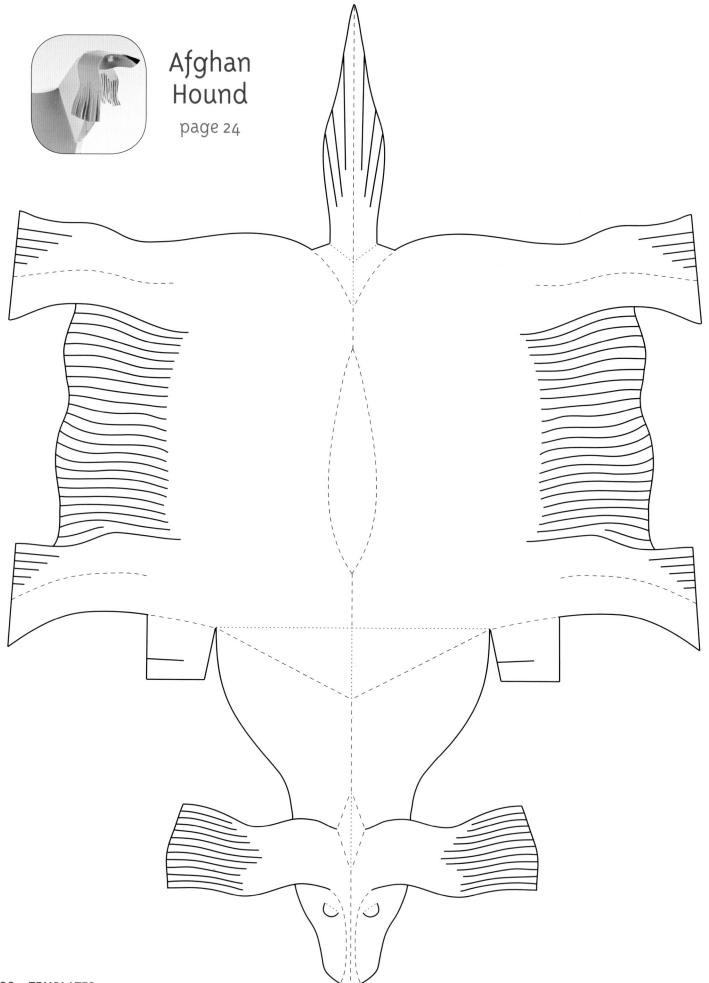

Afghan Hound

page 24

Basset Hound

page 54

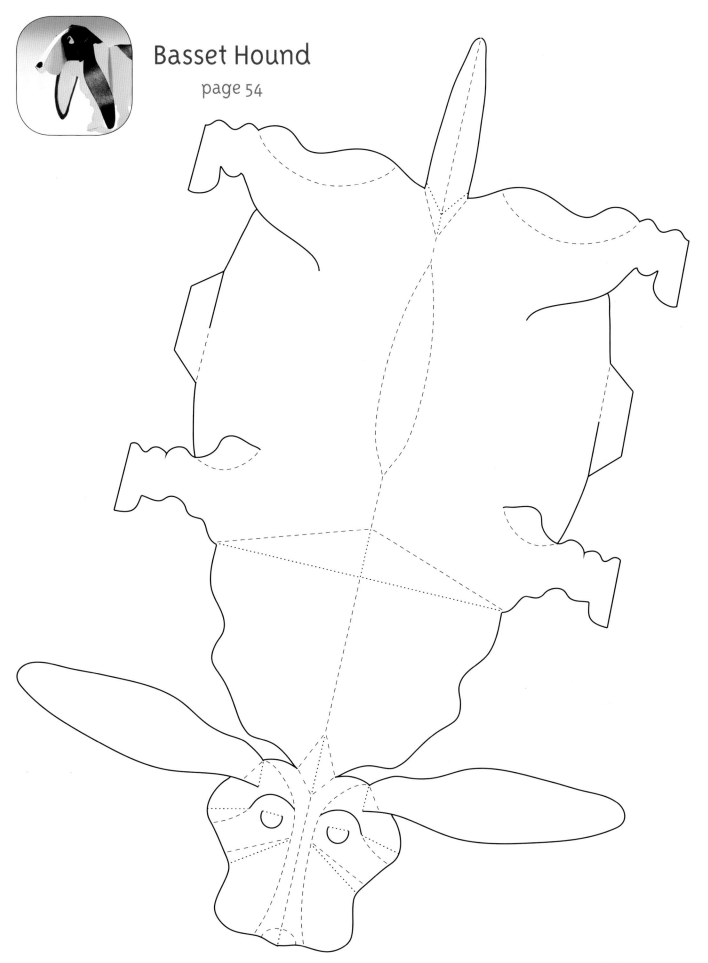

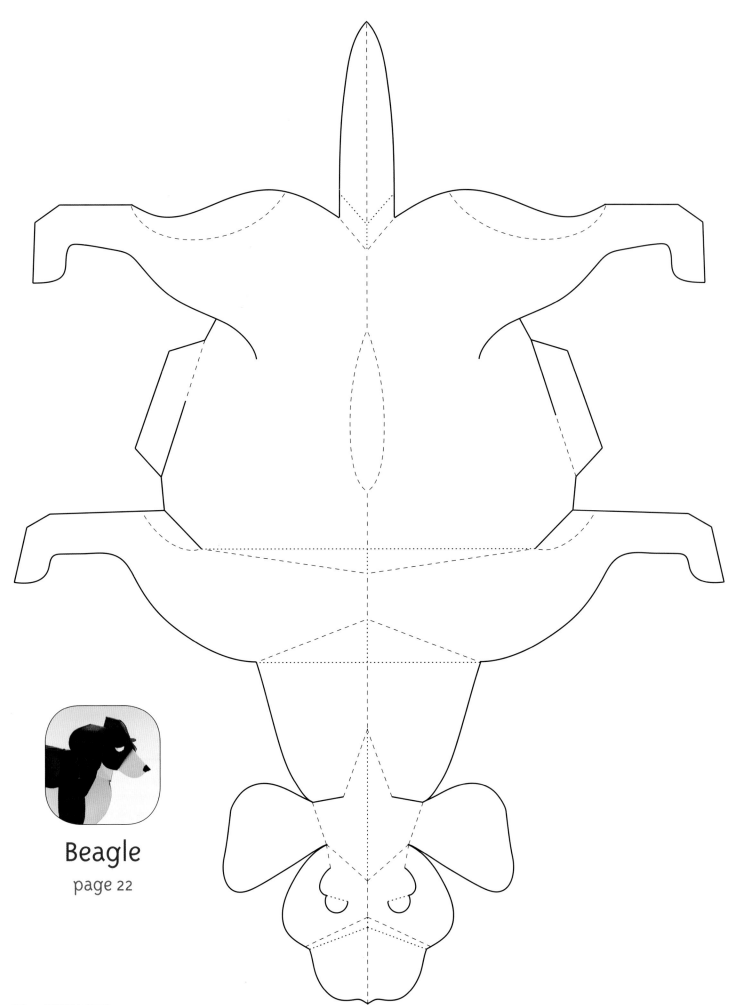

Beagle

page 22

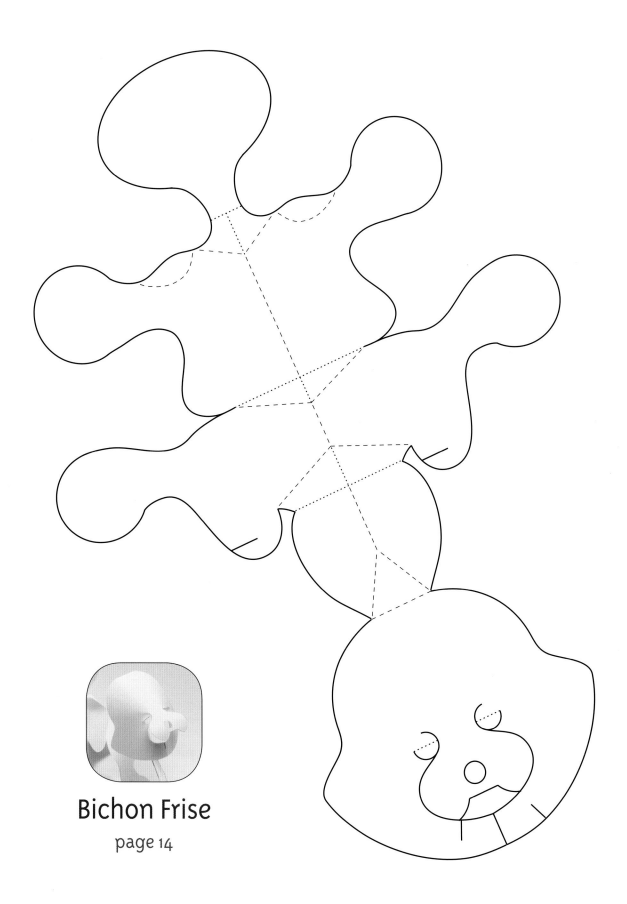

Bichon Frise

page 14

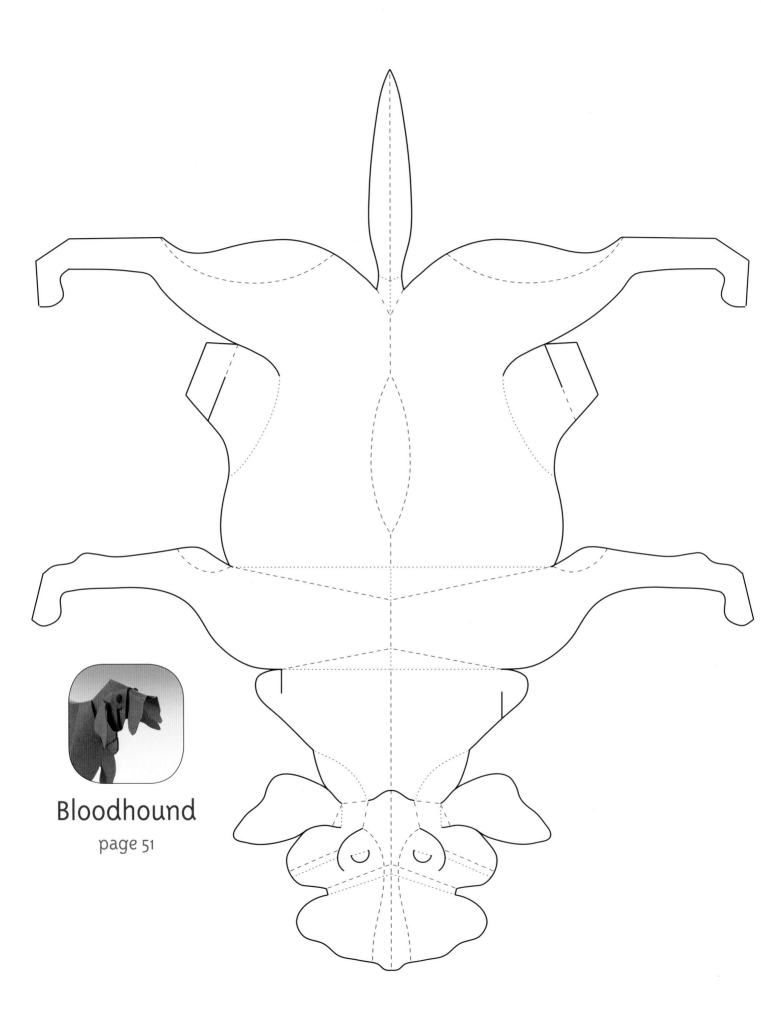

Bloodhound

page 51

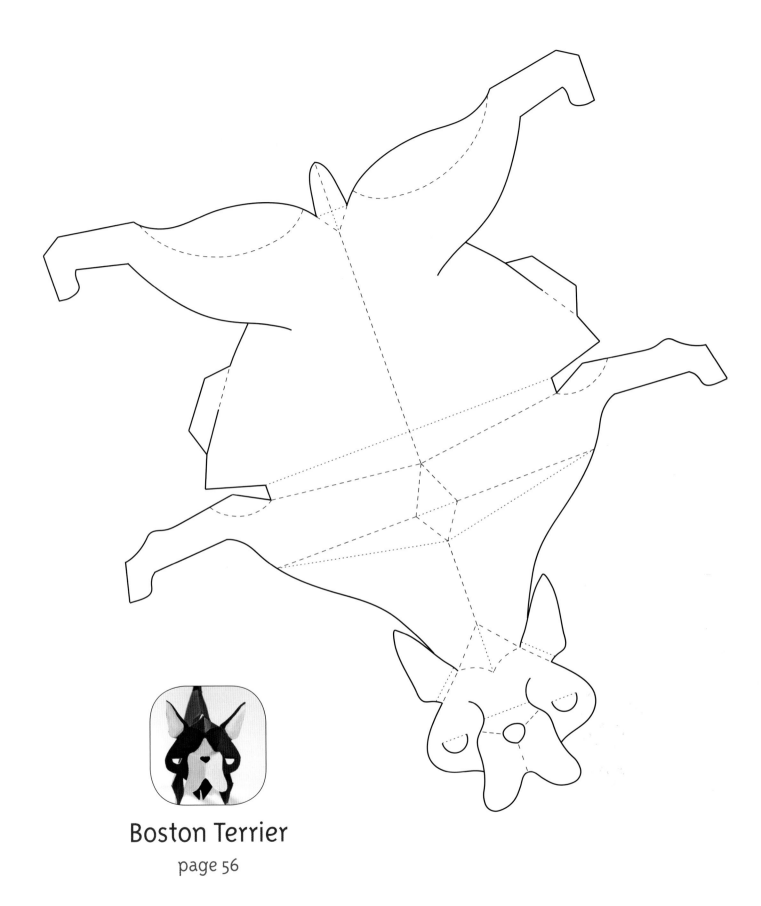

Boston Terrier

page 56

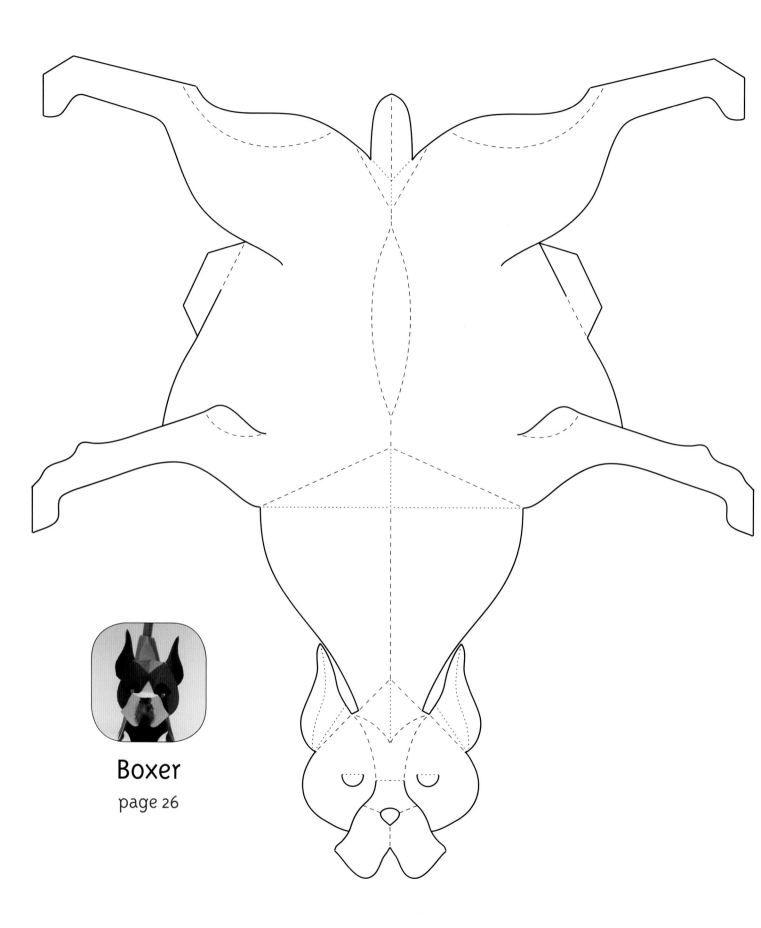

Boxer

page 26

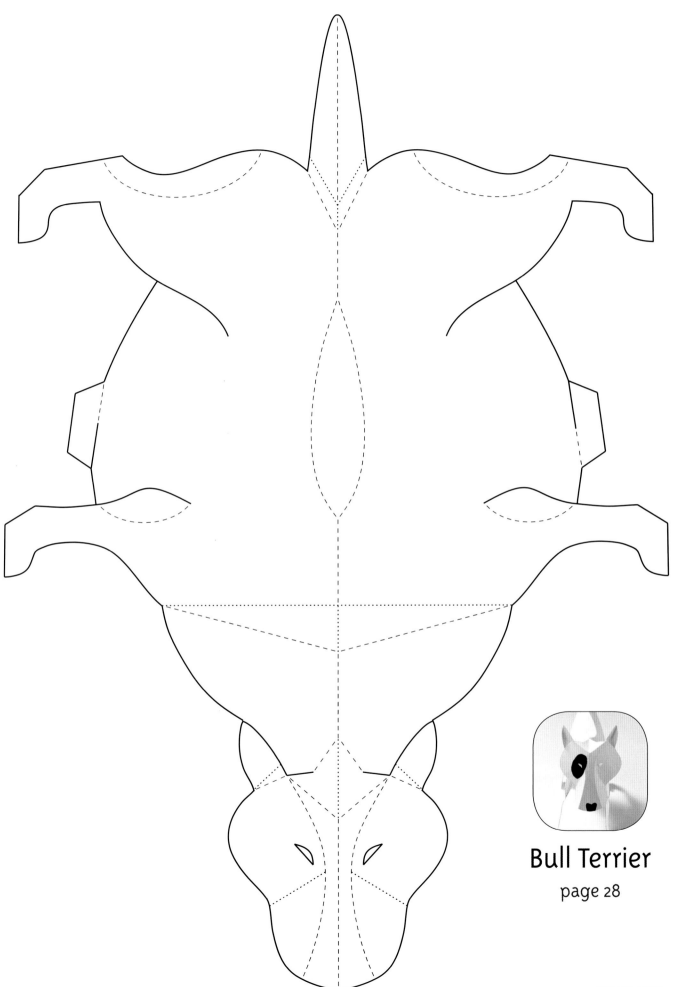

Bull Terrier

page 28

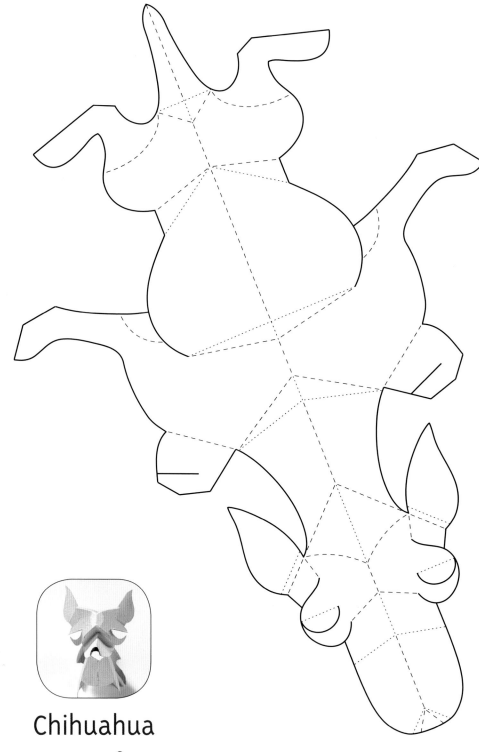

Chihuahua

page 58

Chinese Crested

page 91

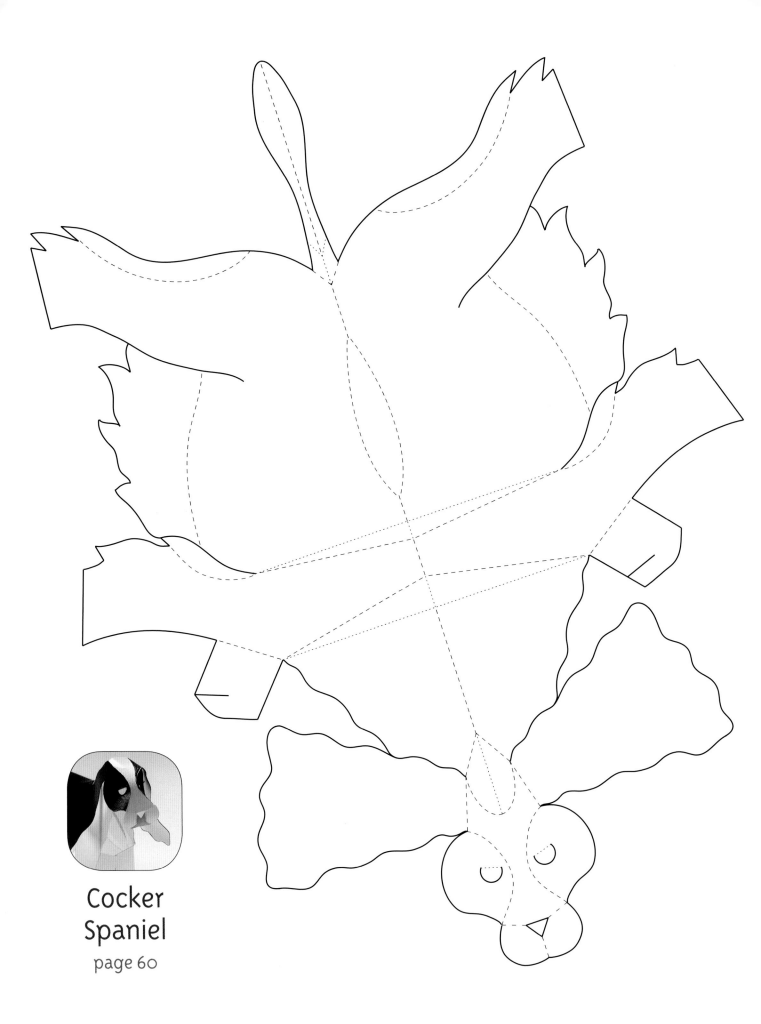

Cocker
Spaniel

page 60

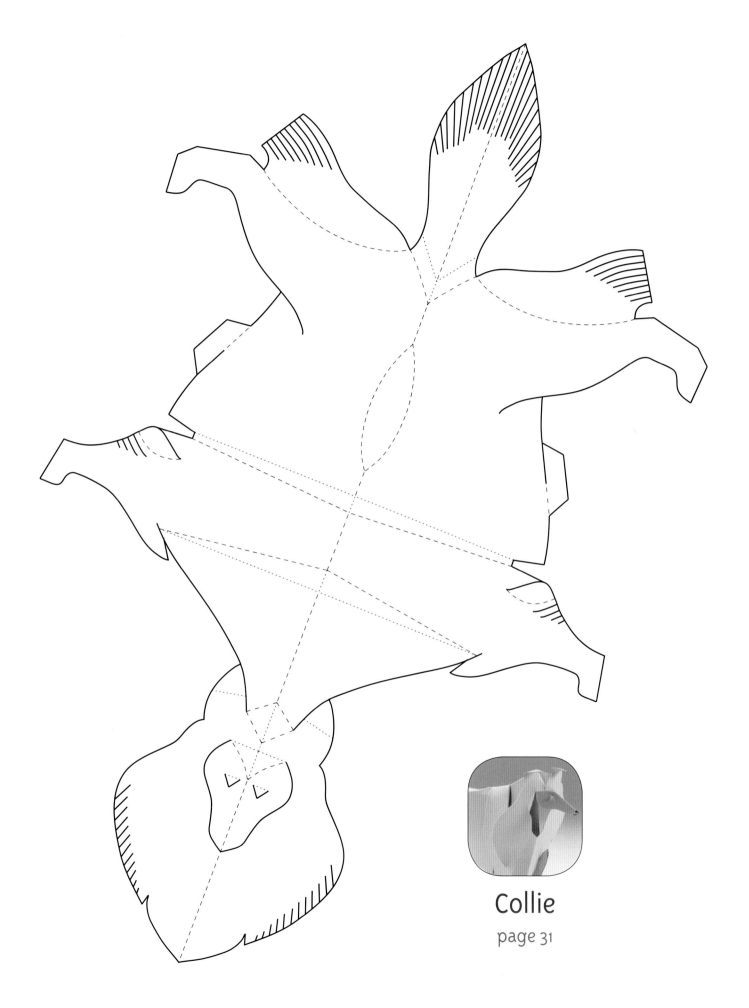

Collie

page 31

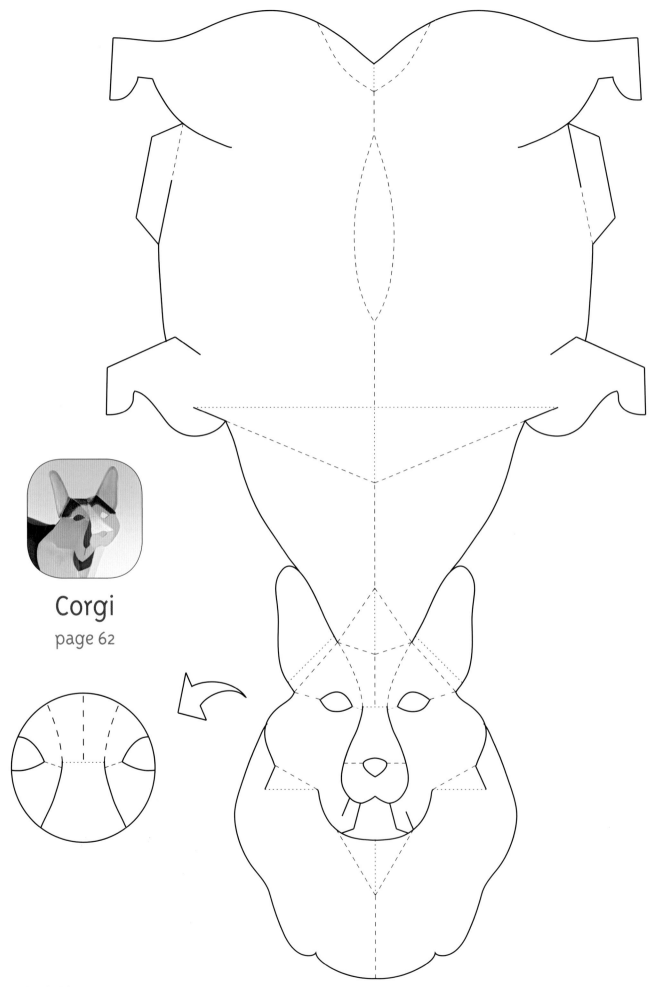

Corgi

page 62

Dachshund

page 34

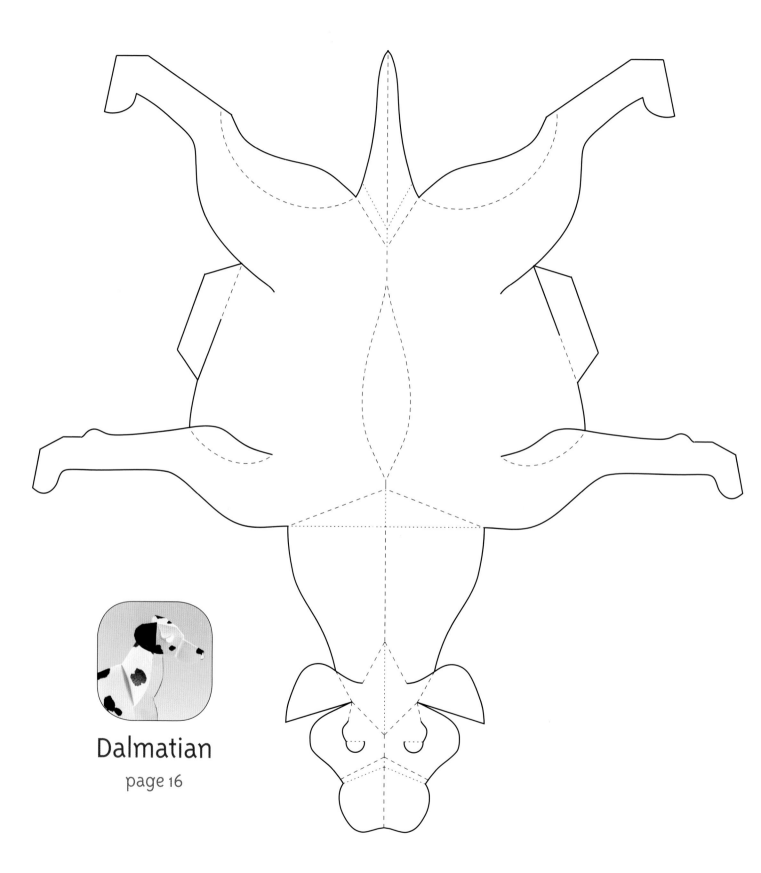

Dalmatian

page 16

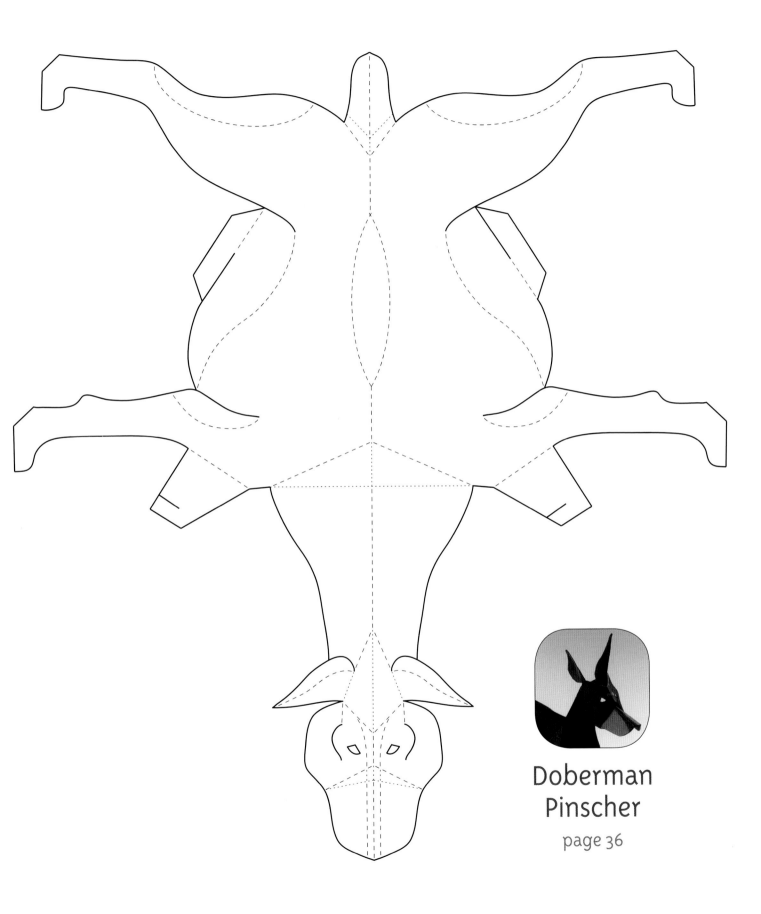

Doberman
Pinscher

page 36

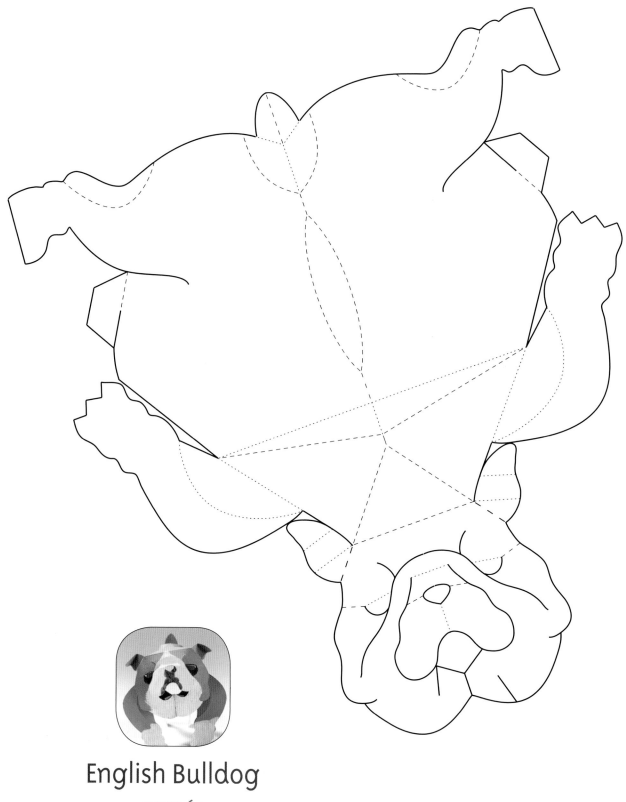

English Bulldog

page 65

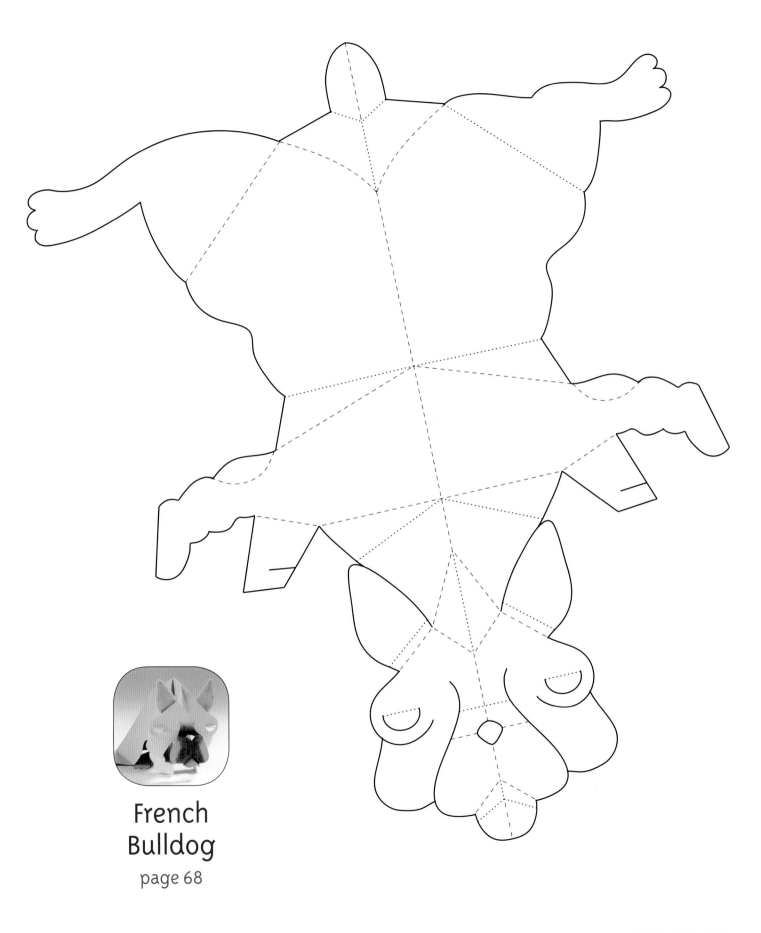

French
Bulldog

page 68

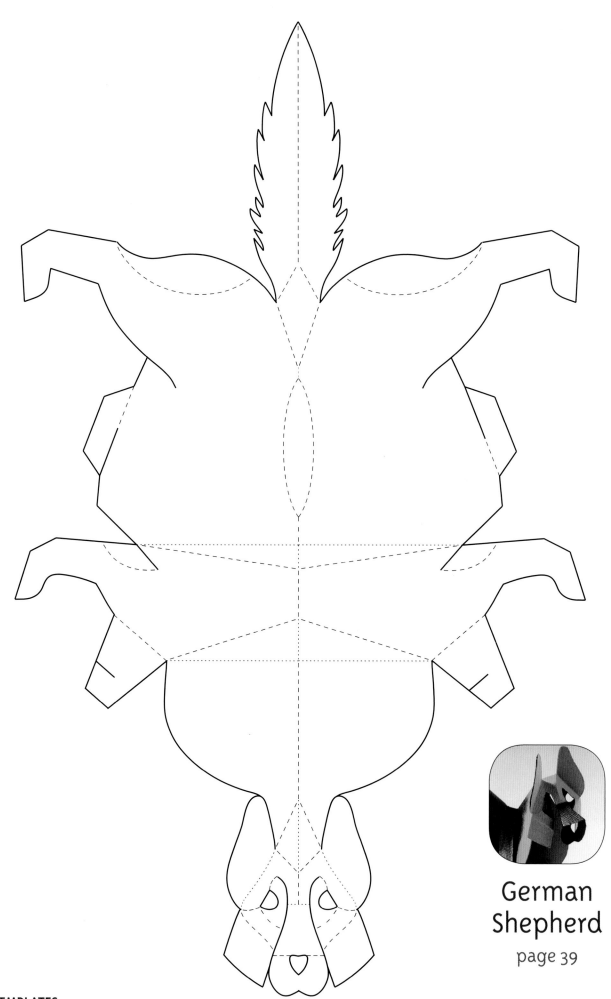

German
Shepherd

page 39

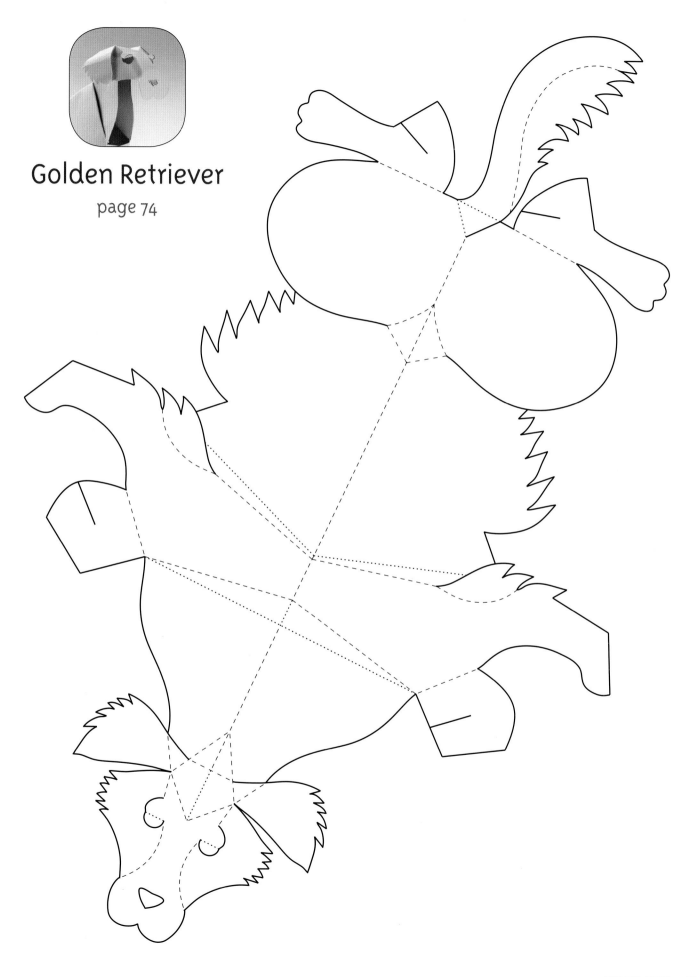

Golden Retriever

page 74

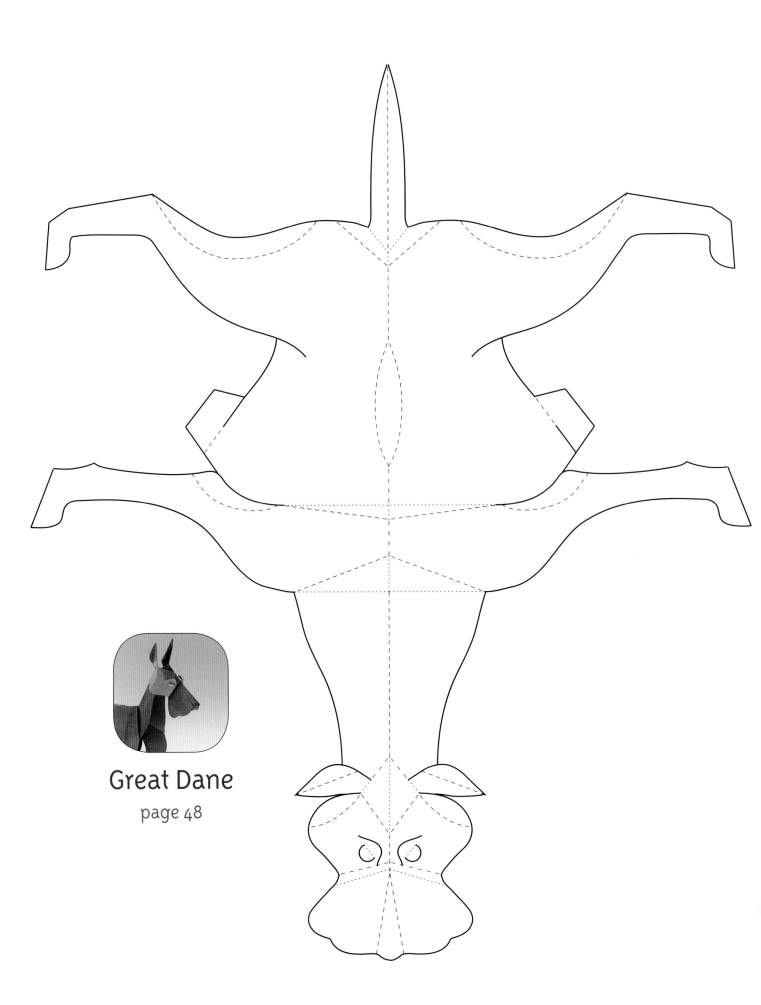

Great Dane

page 48

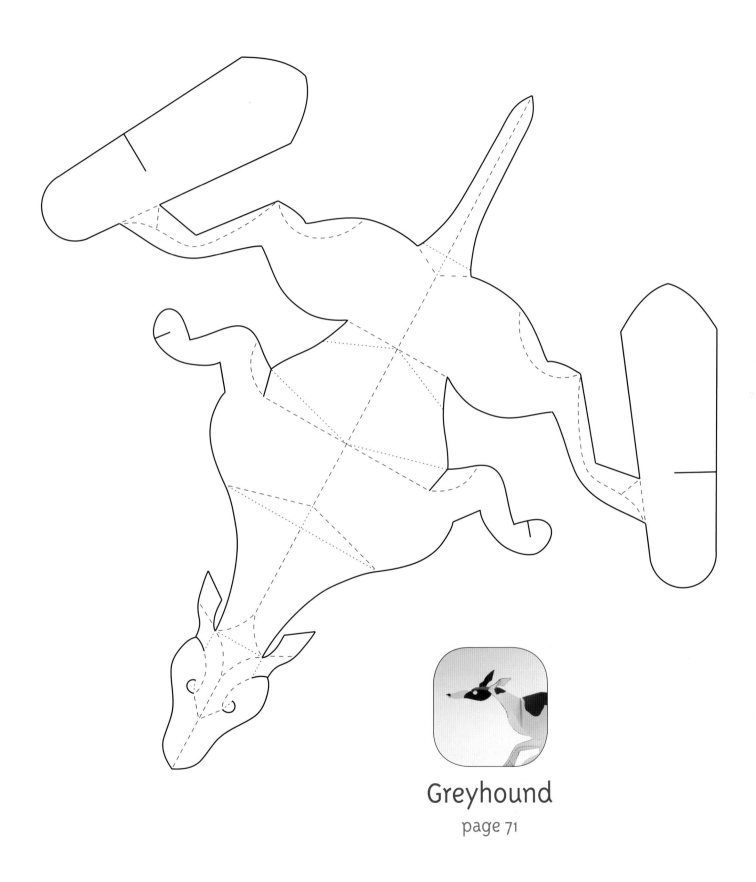

Greyhound

page 71

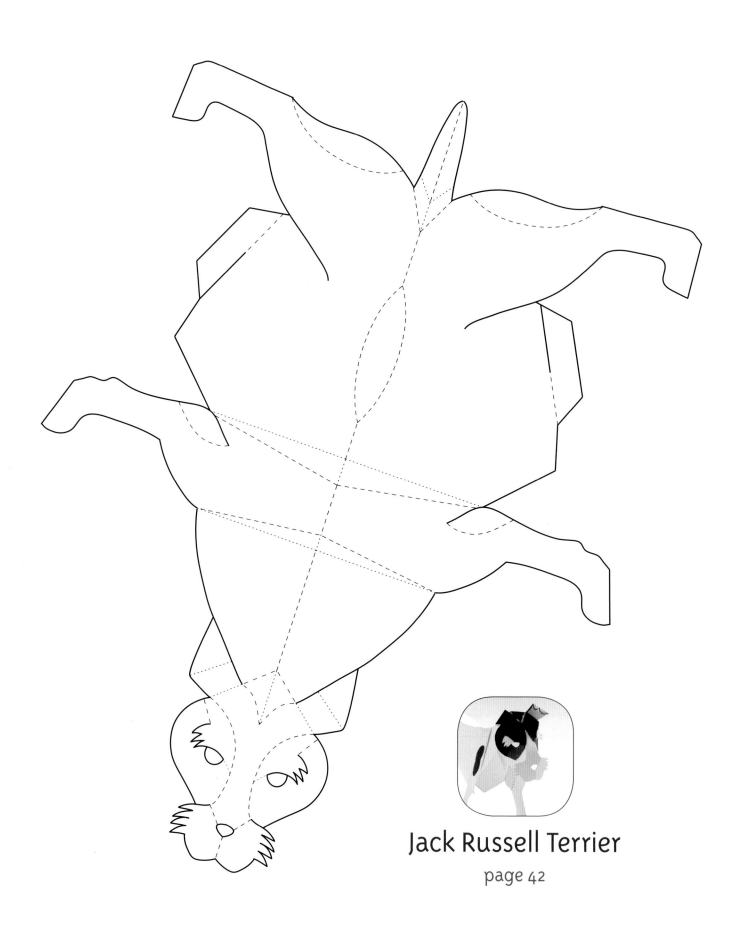

Jack Russell Terrier

page 42

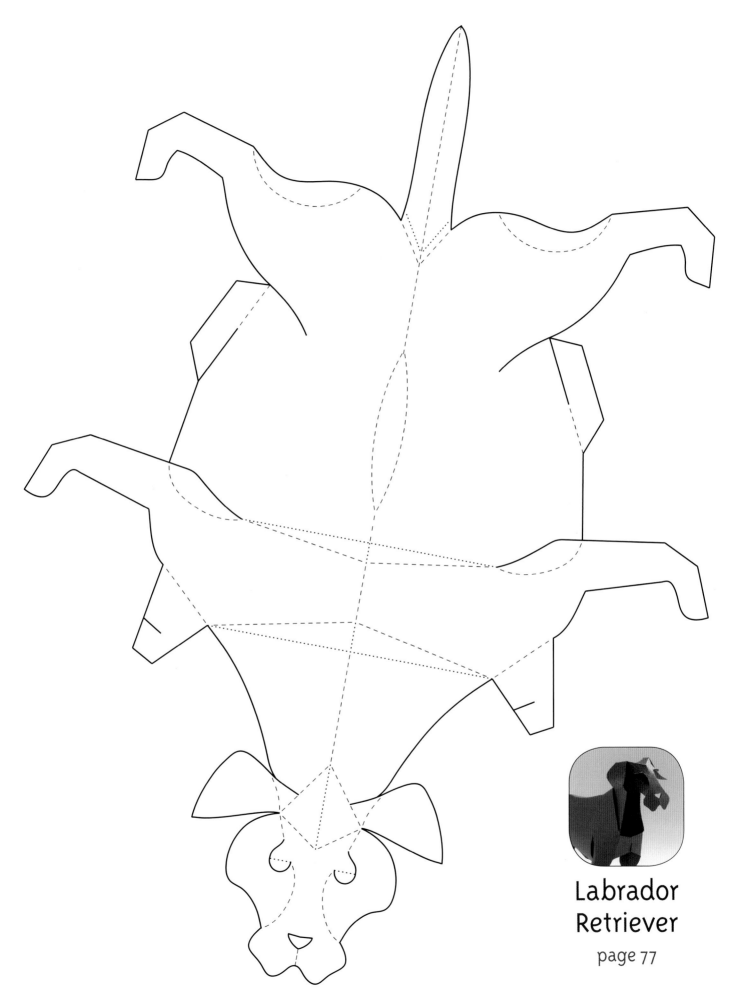

Labrador
Retriever

page 77

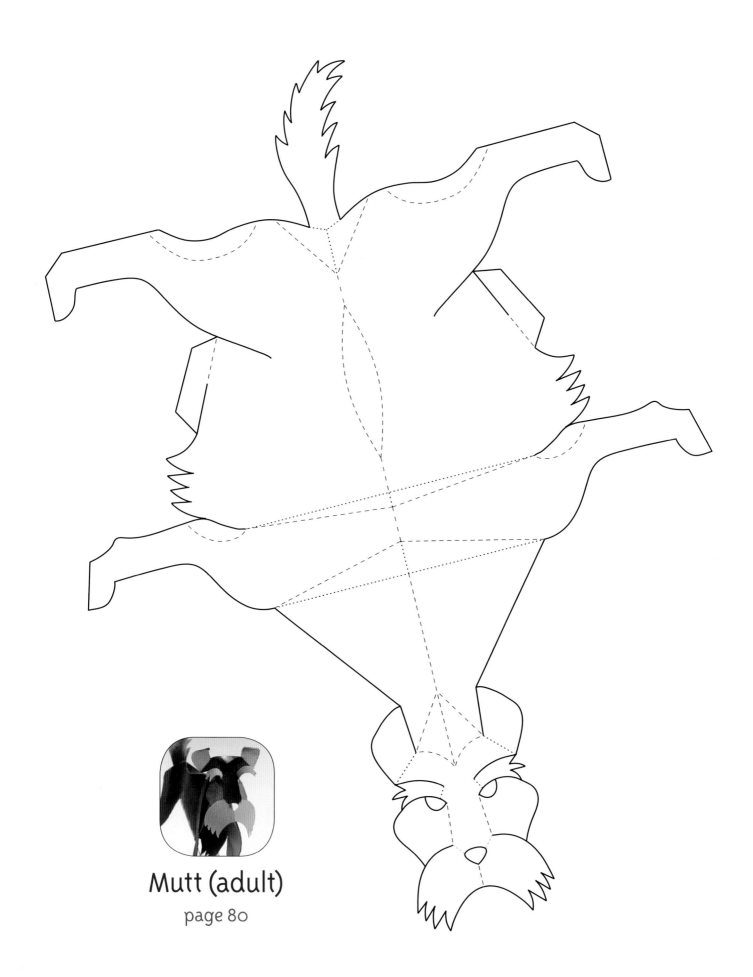

Mutt (adult)

page 80

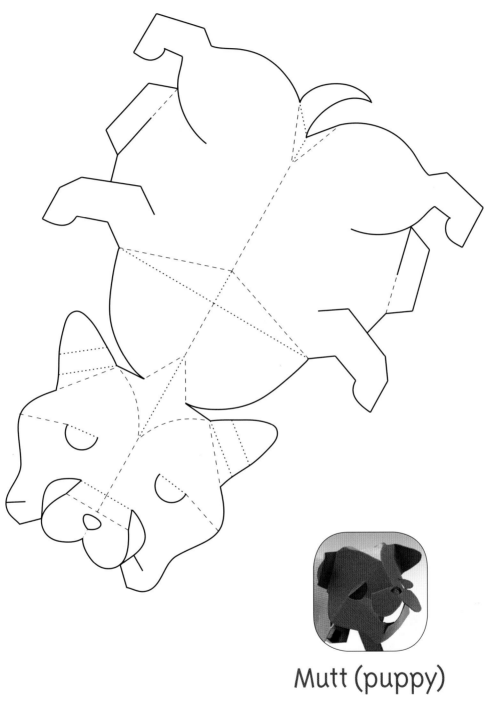

Mutt (puppy)

page 44

Pomeranian

page 82

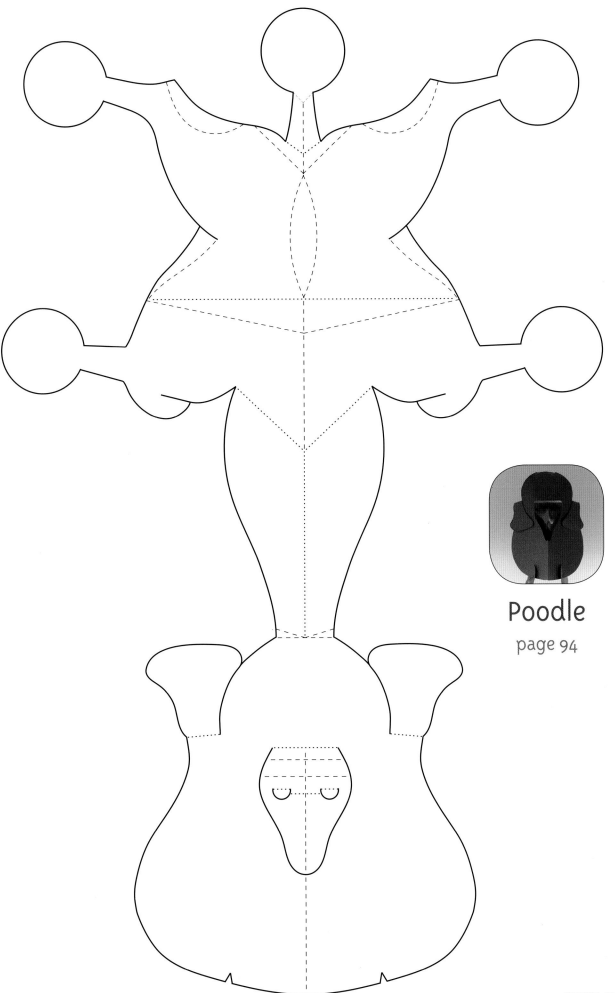

Poodle

page 94

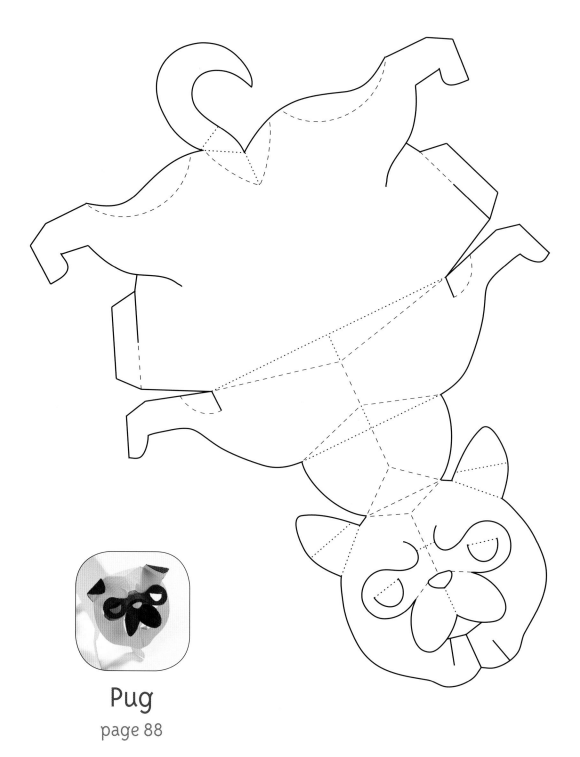

Pug

page 88

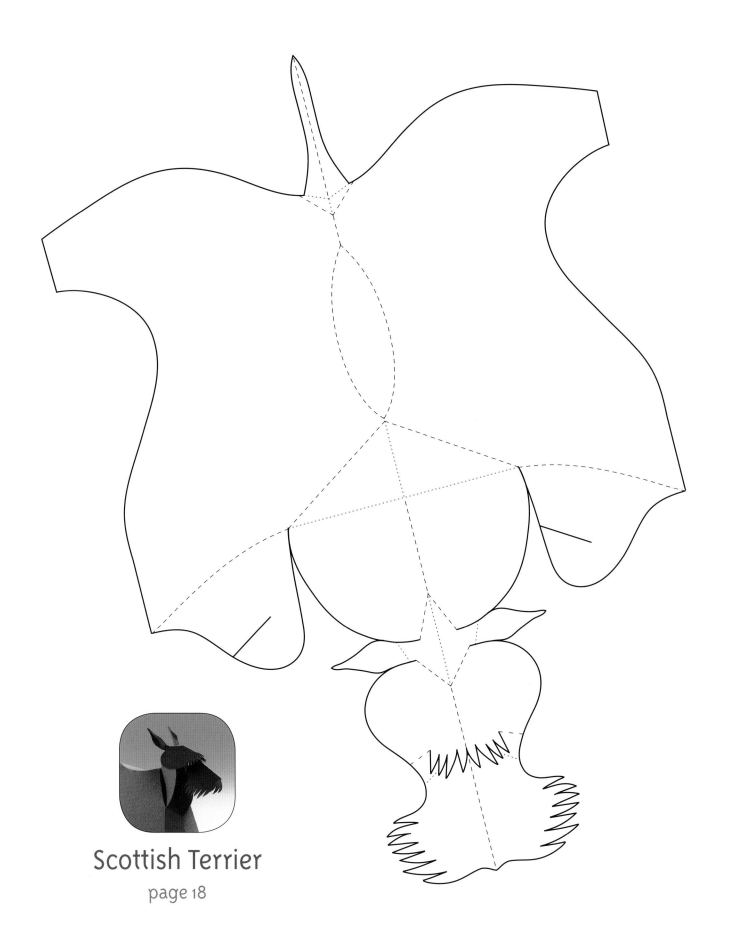

Scottish Terrier

page 18

Shar-Pei

page 96

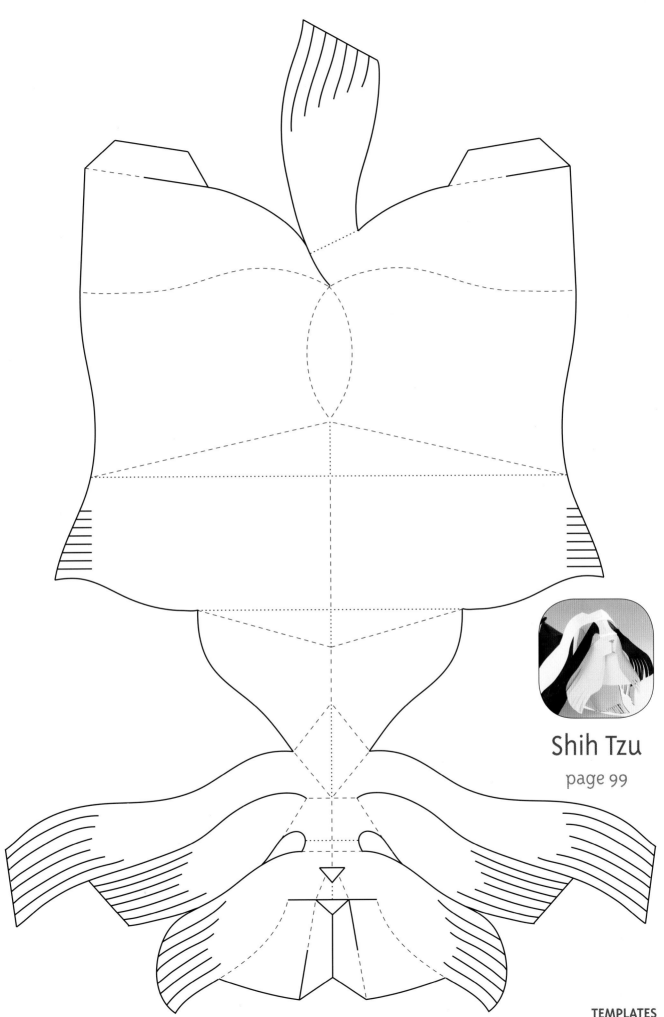

Shih Tzu

page 99

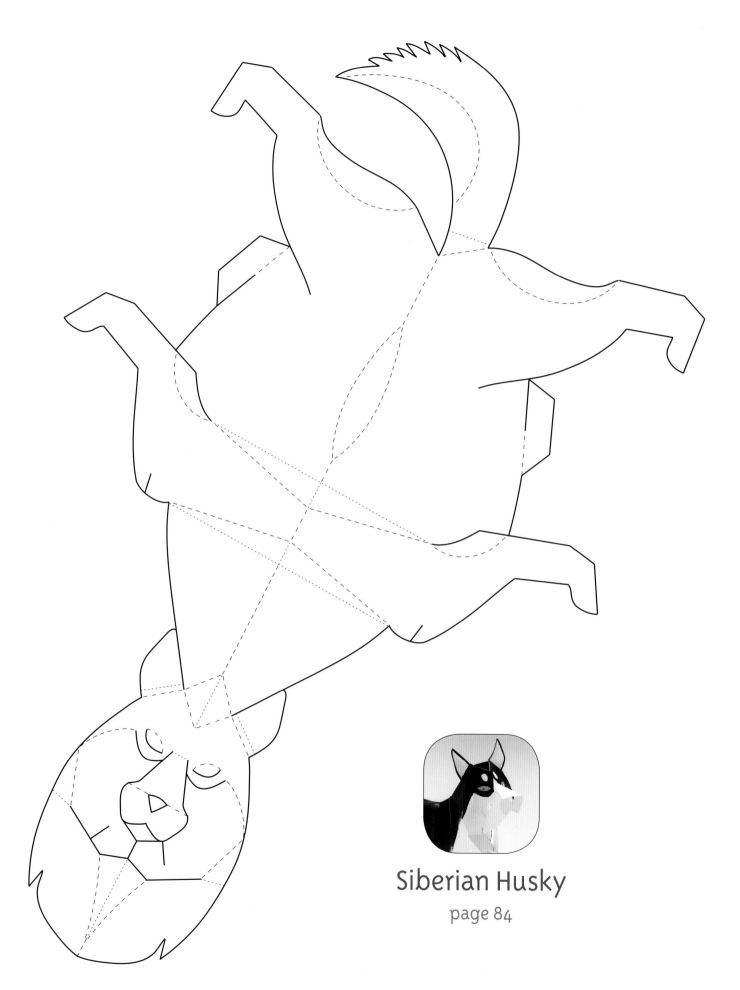

Siberian Husky

page 84

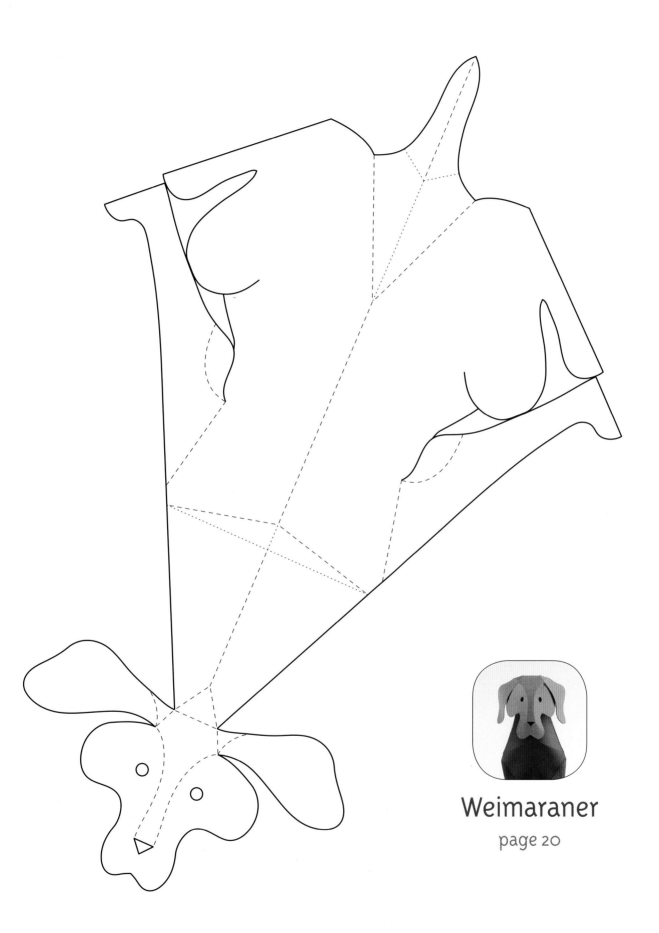

Weimaraner

page 20

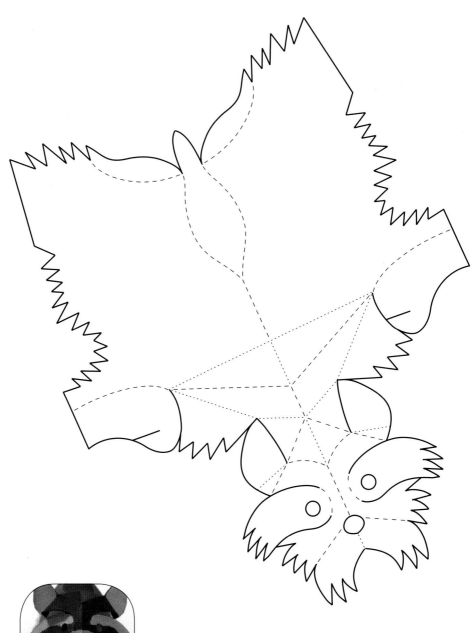

Yorkshire Terrier

page 46

About the Author

Hiroshi Hayakawa was born and raised in Japan. He earned a BA in French literature from Keio University in Tokyo. After a short stint working as a computer systems engineer, he decided his love of life was making art. He relocated to the United States in 1991 and attended Columbus College of Art and Design, earning BFAs in photography and fine arts, and then Cranbrook Academy of Art for his MFA in photography.

Ever since he was very young, he has loved hands-on crafts, especially origami. He would work hours on end making origami projects and turning his desk into a small zoo with many animals or a field of grass populated by various insects. It is safe to say that his lifelong interest in paper craft was nurtured in these early formative years, and it never really went away. He published his first paper craft book, *Kirigami Menagerie*, with Lark Crafts in 2009. This is his second book with Lark Crafts.

He currently lives in Columbus, Ohio, with his wife, Nanette, two cats, three dogs, and a turtle. He teaches at Columbus College of Art and Design and exhibits his art nationally and internationally. His art is represented by Sherrie Gallerie in Columbus, Ohio. You can find his work on his website, www.hiroshi-hayakawa.com.

Editor: **Beth Sweet**
Art Director: **Kristi Pfeffer**
Book Designer: **Michelle Owen**
Illustrator: **Hiroshi Hayakawa**
Photographer: **Steve Mann**
Cover Designer: **Eric Stevens**

Acknowledgments

I would like to express my sincere gratitude to the following people. Without you, this book wouldn't have been possible.

Thank you to all the people at Lark Crafts and Sterling Publishing who contributed to the development of this book.

My special thanks go to:

Nicole McConville for seeing the potential in this project and working to turn it into a reality.

Beth Sweet for your excellent communication and much patience in dealing with me when I kept sending you many many revisions. And to your dog Willow for keeping us company and providing moral support (in the happy growl) during the photo shoot.

Shannon Yokeley for working so hard to make my paper dogs look really good in the photographs. I felt my pups were in good hands.

Tanya Johnson for your assistance in the photo shoot. Your laugh made our job much easier.

Kristi Pfeffer for your excellent art direction and Michelle Owen for your beautiful layout design. My dogs have found a good home in your design.

Karen Levy for your excellent copyediting work. This book flows much more smoothly thanks to you.

Steve Mann for your photographic magic. It was such a joy to work with you for a second time. You rock!

My father, Toshio Hayakawa, and my late mother, Sachiko Hayakawa, for not saying "no" to me every time I asked them to buy me another origami book when I was small.

And my wife, Nanette, for turning me into a dog lover by bringing home the unwanted pug "Puggy" that spring day many years ago. My life hasn't been the same ever since.

Bonus Online Projects

Index

Find seven more paper pup projects and another accessory online at www.larkcrafts.com/bonus.

Chow Chow

Cavalier King
Charles Spaniel

Schnauzer

Puli

Saint Bernard

Long-hair
Yorshire Terrier

Dalmation
Puppy

Basset Hound
Hat and Pipe
(accessory)